Church on the Move

Peter Neilson *has been a minister of the Church of Scotland for over 30 years, in the parish of Mount Florida, Glasgow and later as Associate Minister in the Parish Church of St Cuthbert, Edinburgh. He has also encouraged the evangelistic mission of the church as an Adviser in Mission and Evangelism, Director of Training at St Ninian's Centre, Crieff, and currently in the role of supporting New Charge Developments within Scotland. He convened the special commission which produced the "Church without Walls" report in 2001. He is married to Dorothy with two married daughters, one about-to-be-married daughter and a delightful 2 year old granddaughter.*

The **Chalmers Lectures** *which form the basis of this book were graciously hosted in 2004 by St Mary's College, St Andrews, and New College, Edinburgh. They have also been delivered in the International Christian College, Glasgow in 2005."*

The Chalmers Lectures 2004

Church on the Move

New Church
New Generation
New Scotland

an emerging profile

Peter Neilson

Covenanters

Published by
Covenanters Press
the joint imprint of
Zeticula
57 St Vincent Crescent
Glasgow
G3 8NQ
and
Scottish Christian Press
21 Young Street
Edinburgh
EH2 4HU

http://www.covenanters.co.uk
admin@covenanters.co.uk

ISBN 1 905022 24 7 Paperback

To Dorothy

whose belief in me gives me courage

Contents

Preface

by the Very Rev Finlay AJ Macdonald, Principal Clerk of the General Assembly and Convener of the Chalmers Lectureship Trust.

The Chalmers Lectureship Trust was instituted in 1880 in memory of Rev Dr Thomas Chalmers, the leader of 'the Disruption' and first Principal of New College Edinburgh, where he was Professor of Theology.

Chalmers was one of the leading figures in the early nineteenth century Established Church, promoting the mission of the Church in places of extreme social need, especially in Glasgow. But it was his contribution to the Church's debates on the freedom of the Church in its relation with the civil magistrate that helped to inspire the chain of events that led to the Disruption of 1843.

Chalmers profoundly believed in the principle of Establishment, the Calvinist notion of the civil magistrate's support of the national Church. Even more profound, however, was his belief in the necessary spiritual freedom of the Church; its need to be free from inappropriate interference or control by the secular power. Through his London lectures of 1838, Chalmers' teaching influenced church-state thinking in England as well as Scotland.

In a series of court cases in the late 1830s and early 1840s, the independence of the courts of the Church of Scotland was challenged, and in Chalmers' view compromised, by a number of decisions that set the civil law against the authority of the General Assembly and Presbyteries of the Church. In the Disruption, Chalmers and the hundreds of other ministers who left the Church of Scotland sacrificed the advantages of Establishment for the greater prize of what they saw as a recovery of spiritual independence.

Against that background and in that spirit, the General

Assembly of the Free Church in 1880 received a donation of £5,000 from Robert Macfie Esq. of Airds and Oban for the establishment of a Trust to promote lectures by Free Church ministers or professors on the subject 'the headship of Christ over his Church and its independent spiritual jurisdiction'. In the early years of the Trust, the lectures focussed in part on the principles at the heart of the Free Church's claims, and the doctrine of the nature of the whole Church.

Today, following the reunion in 1929 of the main strands of Presbyterian Church life in Scotland, the Trust is administered through the Church of Scotland; the lecturers include ministers and academics from the Church of Scotland or from traditions in sympathy with its beliefs, and the topics of the lectures have broadened to deal with the general doctrine of the Church and kingdom of Christ.

Recent lecturers have included the late Douglas Murray, whose study of the process leading to the reunion of 1929 (*Rebuilding the Kirk: Presbyterian Reunion in Scotland 1909-1929*, Edinburgh: Scottish Academic Press 2000) is the principal treatment of that subject in print; and Professor Stewart J Brown, whose lectures (*The National Churches of England, Ireland, and Scotland 1801-1846*, Oxford: Oxford University Press 2003) compared the established churches throughout the United Kingdom in the earlier part of the nineteenth century.

November 2004

Foreword

For more than a generation, the churches of Europe have faced a crisis of falling membership and attendance. Carefully documented by sociologists, a rapid decline in patterns of affiliation is evident to anyone over the age of about forty. Gone are the quiet Scottish Sundays of our childhood when shops were closed for business, when streets were deserted, and when the principal social activity was attendance at the 11.00 a.m. service of worship. From its peak of around 1.25m adult members in the late 1950s, membership of the Church of Scotland has been reduced by more than 50%. Today it continues to decline steadily at an average rate of 19,000 per annum. If this trend continues, numbers will halve again in little more than a decade. Unable to replace the dead with new recruits, the Kirk is in danger of becoming largely an institution of the elderly and the middle-aged. If not wholly absent, those in their twenties and thirties are now severely under-represented.

Whether the patterns of secularisation are confined to Europe or representative of a wider global phenomenon is a contested issue amongst social theorists. Is our religious decline the exception or the rule? Recent trends seem to suggest the former. The contemporary world is one in which the forces of religion, whether for good or ill, appear quite resurgent. Even in the USA, the social significance of religion has been powerfully manifested in the 2004 presidential election campaign. Moreover, ours is an age in which Christianity has become a truly global religion, rather than one dominated by its western expressions. Its heartlands now include large stretches of Africa, Asia and Latin America. The recession of the faith in Europe has been matched by an astonishing progression elsewhere, reminding us that the Church has never been consistently represented by one region or people. Its history reveals ebbs and flows, with mission often most effective not at the (self-perceived) centre but at the circumference.

The post-Christian position of the churches of Europe is an ambivalent one. We cannot forget our past, nor ignore the ways in which it continues to impinge upon the present. We have our ancient churches with their patterns of worship. The history of the Scottish nation has been deeply influenced by the beliefs and practice of Christianity, particularly in recent centuries by its reformed and Presbyterian expression. The Church will continue to enact important rites of passages, especially in times of crisis, whether local, national or global. Yet there is no denying that the Church of Scotland is now at a stage where its mission can no longer be conceived in terms of maintaining the protestant identity of the nation. In this respect, the last sentence of Declaratory Article III looks pretty anachronistic.[1] Today, models of evangelism and outreach must be developed if the 'unchurched', those without previous experience and with little comprehension of the faith, are to be reached.

In his Chalmers Lectures, Peter Neilson faces these issues more boldly and imaginatively than most other commentators. His analysis is offered to serve the mission of the Church. Rooted in a theological vision that blends catholic, ecumenical and evangelical themes, his proposals take us deep into the realities of modern culture. One of the strengths of his assessment lies in its capacity not to underestimate the sheer incomprehension of younger people today when faced with the realities of traditional church life – its architecture, forms of worship, and modes of speech. He argues that very different patterns of adherence, worship and nurture will require to be developed in the future if the mission of the Church is to be advanced in Scotland. Supported by reference to studies from other churches throughout the world, this project is cast in 'post-modern' terms, partly in order to accentuate the radical nature of the change that is being demanded of us.

Questions will inevitably arise. Are maintenance and mission really divisible if the transmission of faith to our children remains an important aspect of Christian renewal? How are new initiatives to be funded if not from those more traditional, suburban congregations that currently provide a significant proportion of the Kirk's income? (If they decline or disappear, what then?) Is our ecumenical commitment to the ordained ministry of word and sacrament to be re-affirmed and, if so, how will this be exercised in the coming generation? In what ways is Presbyterianism (and catholicity) to be re-affirmed in the face of more Congregationalist trends? We will have to ponder and debate these issues in the months and years ahead.

Nevertheless, a further merit of Peter Neilson's proposals is to direct our attention again to the local church. It is to the local church that people come for worship, nurture, education and friendship. Within the congregation, the call of God is heard and followed, while resources – spiritual, material personal – are generated for its wider work. And it is from this setting that mission will take place, with people mobilised to do God's will. The published version of these Chalmers Lectures now places in a wider domain this challenging and forthright account of the tasks facing the Kirk in our society. For this, we are greatly in Peter's debt.

Rev David Fergusson,
Professor of Divinity, Head of School
New College, Edinburgh

Introduction

'What kind of church will offer the next generation access to the Gospel?'

This question, both spoken and unspoken, has shaped my ministry in practice and in theological reflection for 30 years in contemporary Scotland. It is the persistent question running through these 2004 Chalmers Lectures.

The Chalmers Lectures have as their primary subject: 'the headship of Christ over his Church and its independent jurisdiction', but the theme may also relate to 'the general doctrine of the church and the kingdom of Christ'. The focus is left to the lecturer. The group commissioning the lectures in 2004 suggested the subject: 'Issues of the church in contemporary Scotland.' This title offered an open field.

These lectures are an invitation to wrestle publicly with my personally challenging question. The question itself is more modest than the rather confident title to the series: *New Church, New Generation, New Scotland – an emerging profile.* Any confidence must lie in the God of the generations, not in my fragmented responses to the persistent question.

The thesis of the lectures is that while the Church as we have known it seems to be losing ground by any of the usual statistical measures, there is another church emerging. The discontinuity between the old and the new is greater than most have recognised. We must not dismiss these movements as maverick or anomalous when compared with our history. We must see them as signs of the Spirit beckoning a church that is only 2,000 years young to move forward into God's new creation. 'The psychology of youth has always been the character of this faith.'[2]

The practical response is an issue of discernment. Will we keep listening to the disappearing church to shape our policies and priorities, or will we find ways of responding to and resourcing the emerging church? What kind of ministry will this emerging church need? What qualities of leadership will be required for such a church? Are we ready to move the investments from shoring up the old to nurturing the new? Responding to these questions requires courageous leadership.

We share the journey of exploring the contours of this new territory through six chapters, but first, we must hear a word or two from the man himself, in whose honour these lectures are commissioned.

The Chalmers' Connection

'Who cares about the Free Church compared with the Christian good of Scotland? Who cares about any church but as an instrument of Christian good? For be assured that the moral and religious well-being of the population is of infinitely higher importance than the advancement of any sect.'[3]

These robust words of Thomas Chalmers remind us of our calling under God as the Church of Jesus Christ in Scotland – that the grace of God may flow to every nook and cranny of our land for the good of the people through the presence of Christian individuals and communities in every aspect of the nation's life.

Chalmers would have affirmed the prayer that has been my prayer for over a decade, the prayer vision of the Board of National Mission of the Church of Scotland, with whom I currently work in the area of supporting new church development:

> *That the people of Scotland in all its parts may hear clearly the gospel of Jesus Christ, see the life of his Spirit among his people and come to know the love of God the Father.*

Thomas Chalmers faced a critical moment in the life of the church in Scotland. We too face a critical time in the church in Scotland. For Chalmers it meant the formation of a new church across the land. For different reasons and in different ways, we see a new church emerging across Scotland. These lectures are an attempt to give one person's profile of that emerging church in the early years of the 21st century.

Chalmers pioneered his missionary initiatives in Glasgow. His ministry in the Tron in central Glasgow (1815-23) gave birth to his vision of the territorial ministry for Scotland – dividing his parish into districts with elders and deacons who cared for the poor. His work for 'pauperism' led to closure of the local workhouse (which cost the city £1,400 per annum), as the Church took up the role. The Church's care system cost only £280 while encouraging dignity and thrift, which, according to one biographer: 'did far more to prevent pauperism than to provide for it.'[4]

The last years of his life were given to earthing this same missionary vision in the West Port of Edinburgh. He wrote:

> *I have determined to assume a poor district of two thousand people, and superintend it myself, though it be a work greatly too much for my declining strength and means. Yet do I hold to be the efficiency of the method of divine blessing, that perhaps, as the concluding act of my public life, I shall make the effort to exemplify what as yet I have only expounded.*[5]

By a strange coincidence (George MacLeod said, 'If you believe that is a coincidence, I wish you a dull life!'), my faith and ministry have been deeply shaped by both these areas of Scotland: in St George's Tron in Glasgow responding to the call of God to give my life to Christ in March 1966, and thirty years later (from 1997-2003) in exploring new patterns of church in the parish church of St Cuthbert in Edinburgh, whose southern boundary is Chalmers' beloved West Port.

These life-shaping encounters with God in worship and in mission shape my observations and my conviction that God is calling out a new church for a new generation in a new Scotland.

Peter Neilson

Chapter One

Church on the Move – a view across Scotland

We are at a critical moment in the life of the Church in Scotland: many people recognise that we are in a time of transition. Some see this situation as the gift of God's moving Spirit and point to many signs of resurrection around the country. Some see it instead as the result of human failings and therefore a call for repentance. For some the issues to be discussed are to do with our changing culture, both national and global; for others these issues are more to do with outmoded church structures – local, regional and national. The truth must lie somewhere in a complex mix of them all.

Membership of the Church of Scotland falls by 19,000 per year. Most people under the age of 40 give church little thought. While a spiritual quest is being expressed in film, music, personal therapies and business management, church is no longer seen as the sole provider of spiritual guidance. Social patterns change around issues of family, sexuality, race relations, gender expectations, genetics and global awareness.

In these times of uncertainty, our existing patterns of church life offer little space for the doubt and dialogue essential for a 'Thomas' generation of questioning searchers and disciples. There are many fine Christian people holding onto the pews by their fingernails – many have just given up holding on.

In the National Census of 2001, over 2 million people claimed allegiance to the Church of Scotland. That statistic offers a challenge: to translate a response of goodwill to the Church into a response to the good news of Christ. On the other hand, it also conceals the large number of 'de-churched' people who have given up on church as we know it.

The Scottish Church Census[6]

The Scottish Church Census was conducted on Sunday 12 May 2002 among the 4,144 churches in Scotland belonging to 49 denominations. 75% of churches are either Roman Catholic or Church of Scotland, 52% of the churches responded.

On that Sunday 570,000 people attended worship. Bearing in mind that this figure was drawn from the 52% of churches who responded, this accounts for 11.2% of the population, compared with 14% in 1994. The average age of church-goers was 47 but for the Church of Scotland it was 51. The projection for 2020 is: 331,000 attending with an average age of 56. There is a significant loss of women over the age of 45, and a massive disconnection from people aged under 45, described as Generation X and Generation Y.

The average age of an Elder is 56, while the average (for those over 25) in the general population of church-goers is 51. Three-quarters of churches have no leaders under 35. Handover to smaller and younger teams therefore seems to be essential – begging the question of whether such leadership might even be available.

Churches are in touch with 102,000 young people under 25 through midweek church activities, but this represents only 6.6% of the population under 25. The Christian Research Association describes Generation Z, children born after 2003 in these stark terms:

> *Perhaps a fifth to quarter will be baptised in a church, and a similar proportion will marry in a church. But for the majority, the inside of a church will be as unknown as a castle dungeon.*[7]

The gap between midweek relationship and Sunday worship is still seen as a measure of success or failure. The key will lie in beginning where the young people are … and staying there! We are only just waking up to the possibility of the new working in partnership alongside the old.

As a minister of the Church of Scotland, I am committed to a vision of the grace of God for all in our nation. As a mission facilitator within the Church of Scotland, I wish to challenge the assumed strategy for fulfilling that vision as being only through territorial parish ministry.

Our fundamental shift must be from exclusive territorial mission to cultural and generational mission. A parish church does not mean a parish is churched. We need a mixed economy of Christian community and Christian communication to engage with our nation across the generations.

Not only Scotland…

This story is repeated throughout the Western World. In *The Prodigal Project,* three New Zealanders comment on the sense of exclusion about church felt by many Western Christians, let alone unbelievers.

> *There is something interesting happening in the Christian community across the Western world. Very quietly and unobtrusively, one group of believers is growing on a daily basis. Soon the numbers will be such that they cannot be ignored.*
>
> *Who are they? They are the Christians who don't go to church anymore. The ones who've given up altogether. A recent e-mail from a friend anguished over these missing faces: 'I tell you, so many of my Christian friends – the ones who were going to put the Church to rights, the ones who were going to fight the cause of the disenfranchised believers – are giving it all up now. Not the faith as such. Most of these people still believe in Jesus, and struggle to live a life of discipleship. But they do it on their own, away from congregations and church structures.*[8]

That statement ought to be enough to warn us away from thinking we can make a few easy adjustments to church as we know it to meet the challenges of the missing generations. How many ministers have been brave enough to survey their congregations to find out if the weekly diet of worship and preaching is nourishing the people?

From across the Atlantic we hear language that is equally strong from Loren Mead of the Alban Institute:

> *The storm buffeting the churches is very serious indeed. Much more serious than we have admitted to ourselves, and much more serious than our leaders have yet comprehended... The storm is so serious, I believe, that it marks the end of business as usual for the churches and marks the need for us to begin again building the church from the ground up.*[9]

Church under Review[10]

The research leading to the publication of the *Church without Walls* report unveiled a raft of issues of deep concern about the state of the Church as experienced by many people. Membership of the Church of Scotland has fallen by 19,000 per year for the past 20 years to just below 600,000 out of a population of 5 million – an adult population of around 3 million. 180 of our 1,200 churches have no minister at present, with a consistent gap between recruitment and retirement despite encouraging increases in new processes of enquiry and assessment. This is leading to the belated response of Area Team Ministry which some people perceive to be more about reactive financial expediency than proactive mission strategy.

Over half our congregations need to be financially supported by the generosity of other congregations. Vacancy procedures are unduly protracted. Presbytery patterns of supervision are often too little, too seldom, too late. In an age of participative democracy, decision-making in congregations, Presbyteries and Assembly still leaves many people without a voice.

In many places old ways are just not working. People are being bored out of our churches. Congregations have become obsessed with survival and die from lack of honesty and imagination. Ministers are being destroyed by false expectations of congregations. Others destroy their congregations by their inappropriate expectations and inept handling of people. Basic courtesies and communication are often lacking. The passion for mission and evangelism is massively absent.

Presbyteries have lost their core purpose to support congregations in their work. Decision-making styles eliminate creative people and processes. Representation in wider leadership is often limited by times and patterns of meetings which exclude our ablest people. Systems of visitation and supervision require radical overhaul to establish relationships of trust and mutual support, carried out by adequately qualified people. Elders with management skills speak of being patronised and scandalised by the way Presbytery visits are sometimes handled.

National work is carried forward by a system that grows suspiciously larger as the numerical church becomes smaller. Perceptions of over-centralisation lead to local cynicism and even paralysis of action. Current structures limit cooperation and carry inherited priorities and financial resources. Attempts to refocus central structures meet with embedded resistance. Media coverage confuses people and undermines public credibility.

People in areas of multiple deprivation are often doing more with less, but speak of a 'tale of two churches' where a handful of Christians struggle against incredible odds, while others live with a comfortable supply of people and money. The call is out for a redistribution of resources. In the rural areas where small congregations are often sharing ministry in a multiple linkage, it is still possible to feel neglected and overlooked.

Meanwhile the Church of Jesus Christ is alive and well. Our partner churches around the world remind us that we are part of vast and fast growing movement, representing one third of the world's population. We are reminded by our history that the Church of Jesus Christ has been born, died and been resurrected in many cultures at many different times. We are reminded biblically that the Church is a gift of God's grace, not an invention of human foibles – strangely fragile, yet ultimately indestructible. However we face these critical moments, it must not be with anxiety, but with faith, hope and love.

Around the Church there are many who recognise the moment and call for change. From some the call has come for theologically grounded spiritual renewal and a new Reformation. From others the call is for changes in the patterns of organisation and decision-making. There are many voices calling for change, but experience tells us that we are less enthusiastic about specific proposals when they may affect us personally.

Change begins with a sense of discontent. That discontent is now widespread. The need is then for a vision of a new future. Fresh vision offers fresh energy.

The Emerging Church: A Photomosaic

Vision is a tricky word. One person's vision is another person's guilt trip. When vision is a gift of grace, it comes from God's people recognising the grace of God at work. We see what God is doing and we join in.

In the midst of exile the prophet Isaiah floated words of hope from God: *Behold I am doing a new thing. Now it springs up. Do you not perceive it?*[11] In that spirit of prophetic hope and encouragement we offer a brief photomosaic of the emerging church, and offer an invitation to join in.

Around the country new patterns of church are emerging. Worship takes many forms in many different places led by a wide range of people. For some the cathedral style liturgy offers stability and mystery. For some the bustle of the generations allows relaxed space for all ages. For some it is the reflective space of the gentle arts of story and artistic creativity or walking the ancient Labyrinth of Chartres Cathedral, transposed to local churches. For some the gifts of computer and video technology create multimedia worship spaces for the computer generation.

Worship is not only about content, but about setting the context for our encounter with God. Worship leaders recognise the importance of 'being curators of the worship space'[12] where we may meet God through Jesus Christ. Variety of venue and variety of menu is essential for a choice-based society.

Children's work moves away from Sunday morning and appears in breakfast clubs and after-school clubs, while in many places children find a new place in the church family in Sunday worship. Some churches have grasped the need to rebuild the Church organically 'from the crèche up'. Young people, though fewer, are finding their voice in the Youth Assembly and within the courts of the Church.

Those who are impatient with old forms of church are beginning to invent church for their own generation. These fresh expressions will never be assimilated into an 'inherited' church which can never expand its culture widely enough to include them. The way of integration must be matched by the way of innovation, fostering, in parallel, churches linked into networks of mutual support.

The Christian Research Association suggests that across the UK the over 50s may be finding their way back to church, wanting to offer the time and energy they did not have in their middle years. Experienced women and men in their 'third age' volunteer to go overseas.

Patterns of church leadership are changing too. Kirk Sessions think more as teams than courts. New elders are eager to be trained in pastoral skills; sharing faith, teamwork and leading worship. Staff teams rather than solo ministers are becoming more frequent. Local cooperation with other churches in mission and evangelism takes many forms: from occasional activities to formal covenanted relationships and parish groupings. Area team ministry is becoming a reality in many parts of Scotland.

One church invited twelve people to commit to a year's formation to develop a team which would lead worship, share in pastoral care, develop mission and small group ministry. Why has so much ministry over so many years failed to offer that level of empowerment? The example of Jesus Christ was 'take, teach, test, take, teach, trust'. Instead we simply 'teach, teach, teach, teach, teach, teach… and hope for the best!'

Styles of leadership and decision-making are changing, often through the influence of women whose approach is more naturally participative and nurturing than the male. New patterns of democracy and new styles of business management are cracking the old systems. We are learning how to listen together that it 'may seem good to the Holy Spirit and to us'.[13]

People are coming to faith through paths to discipleship carefully laid down in the life of the congregation. Alpha courses, Emmaus courses and other patterns of faith accompaniment are helping people find living and deepening encounters with Jesus Christ. The searching spirituality of prayer and quiet retreat offers sanctuary from the stresses of life. The Bible is becoming a more open book as people rediscover its unique wisdom through story and 'emotional exegesis',[14] as well as exposure to systematic bible teaching, contextualised expository preaching or the discipline of the common lectionary.

Buildings are being refitted to the 21st century, creating more flexible space for a congregation that wants to become a community at worship and in fellowship – and becoming more accessible for a congregation that wants to be of service to the community around it. Our physical spaces embody our vision of God. Every building tells a story of God. Sometimes its story shouts louder than our story. If resources are to be released for mission, many buildings must be closed. Strategically placed buildings must be refurbished to meet the expectations of people who live in and experience a 21st century service economy.

Repitching the Tent[15] by Richard Giles has been the inspiration both for the reshaping of Renfield St Stephen's (after the collapse of the steeple), and for St George's West, Edinburgh, whose sanctuary was reshaped for community worship rather than simply continue as a preaching centre.

Having a parish church does not mean that the parish is churched. Variety of menu and variety of venue are essential for a society that is fragmented, mobile and living the 24/7 week. We are seeing the development of dispersed church for a diverse culture. Smaller flexible expressions of church are emerging which major on relationships: nurturing our relationships with God, with each other and with the community around us.

Justice is higher on the agenda of many, judging from the massive response to issues such as debt relief or concerted efforts to eliminate homelessness. Phrases like 'social inclusion' have raised questions of how hospitable or otherwise we are, as the Church of Jesus Christ, to those whom he would call friends.

The Church in a multicultural Scotland has entered a new era of relationship with society and civic authorities, both with the advent of the Scottish Parliament and new patterns of health care, education and social policy. In issues of education, social concern and political debate, the Church aims to contribute to the total health of the nation as servant and evangelist, partner and prophet.

The Church that follows the Christ 'through whom and for whom all things were created' is renegotiating its contribution to policy shaping, community health and investment in our children's future. The Church's unheralded contribution to the 'social capital' of the nation has been quantified in the recent research by the Urban Studies Department of Glasgow University.[16]

Increasingly these roles are shared among partner churches of different traditions. The Church of Scotland has been described as having the 'charism of a big heart' – a generous description that re-calls her to be a church marked by the grace of our Lord Jesus Christ. Inspiring examples of ecumenical work are to be found in Barrhead, Carluke, Drumchapel and many other places. Even if the depth and breadth of ecumenical work across the nation has been insufficient to produce the critical mass to carry forward proposals for organic union, local partnerships continue to grow. The Church of Scotland is guardian of a vision of the gospel for every part of Scotland, but that vision can only be a reality in missionary partnership.

In our globalized world, where 51% of the world Church is now in the South and only 3% of the world Church is Presbyterian[17], we take a humbler role in the world and accept the gifts of 'reverse mission'. Environmental concerns and economic imbalances link us and challenge us to make new lifestyle choices in a global context. Global media networks of television, internet and telecommunications bring the Aids crisis of Africa to our doorstep and demand a local response. Our neighbour is African.

A photomosaic is a big picture made up of lots of little pictures, some almost too small to see. While this picture of the Church is made of up small instances of what is emerging, and may be only barely recognisable to some, it is nonetheless possible to visit instances of each of these features in the Church in Scotland today. They may be dismissed as anomalies, or they may be welcomed as signs of God's future Church. We believe that these express a mood for change that is the beginning of a movement for change.

A Movement for Change?

The picture emerges of a church that thinks smaller rather than bigger, but that can be a creative 'mustard seed' minority. Churches may be fewer and older with less time and energy for church work, but they are discovering the ability to be more relational, flexible and provisional. This may be taking us to a situation that is truer to our identity as agents of God's kingdom.

According to J L Segundo, 'it is the situation of Christendom that represents a distortion, or at least an abnormal condition, in the understanding of the Church's role in history. The normal condition and the one that is coming back into focus today is that of a creative minority dedicated to the service of the vast majority'.[18]

We sense ourselves part of a movement – a church on a journey – rather than a settled church for settled community. Here are people who are hearing the call of Jesus: 'Follow me'. To follow involves our feet as well as our hearts and our heads.

The Celtic renaissance has fuelled this movement with its recovery of pilgrimage. Ray Simpson of Lindisfarne sees in the emerging church the marks of roots – connecting with rich traditions; rapport with deeply engrained culture – yet being at home in the new; rhythm – patterns of prayer and action.[19]

The emphasis is shifting from quantity to quality. Build up people in Christ and let God build his Church. People are asking how *coming* to church equips them to *be* the Church in family or work. How can the Church become a *family centre* that strengthens family life 'from the crèche up' and sows seeds of stability for tomorrow's society? How can congregations that claim to be concerned about justice 'out there' become *communities of integrity* that help members live the Sermon on the Mount in today's world?

There is a move from congregation to community: the rediscovery of the cell as the basis of belonging and discovering the gift of friendship in the 'Friends' generation. The Celtic Monastery has been described by Ian Bradley[20] as offering three dimensions: nurturing the heart, offering a home and becoming a hub to equip people for mission in daily life. If churches aspire to be places of heart, home and hub, there we have a metaphor for transformation.

Such churches are being built by teams rather than individuals, with ministers, elders and other staff operating as partners in ministry and mission. Only a community can communicate the gospel. Only a team can build a community. Where there are partners in ministry and mission, isolation is broken and a new synergy is released.

The starting point for reshaping the Church is local rather than central – and that is endorsed most vocally by those who service the 'centre' as a service to local congregations from Shetland to Stranraer. We are witnessing upside down thinking. The bureaucratic church of the 19th and 20th centuries will not survive as it is into the 21st century. It must become local and relational, with regional support and minimum central servicing.

The context of church is global rather than narrowly national. This global dimension has been part of the unfolding missionary story of the Church for 2,000 years. Today world travel is easy. New generation Christians have not only heard of other lands and cultures, many have visited and experienced them at first hand. Parochial attitudes to church will be too confining for a generation who travel widely and see the world.

The future Church will face the rich-poor divide and enjoy the partnership of both young church and older churches. Globalisation affects every local church. Generation Z, born after 2003, are growing up with the internet as the medium for shopping, entertainment and intellectual stimulus. Web-design is becoming a core ministry for future evangelism in the 'dotcom' generation.

There is celebration of diversity and less desire to impose conformity. A pluralist society will require a pluriform church served by a multi-disciplinary team. The history of Christianity has always been marked by fragmentation and with that, competition. Our future can redeem the intransigence of historical difference into an intentional missionary strategy to offer the gospel to different people in different ways in different places. Linked charges need not be locked into inherited identities, but work to offer distinctive but collaborative ministries for the future. Ecumenical diversity can become evangelistic opportunity.

New Churches for a New Scotland

We believe that a new Church is emerging, but will it be a Church that will fit the contours of the new Scotland?

One icon of the 'new Scotland' is the new parliament at Holyrood, a symbol of Scotland's new identity as we move into the 21st century. Putting aside the controversy surrounding the Holyrood building, the Scottish Parliament is a symbol of a watershed in Scotland's new self-confidence, new self-awareness and new sense of place in the world. What is the calling of the Church of Jesus Christ in this context?

According to sociologist, David McCrone,[21] Scotland is the first truly post-modern nation – not based on a narrow ethnic identity, but on a democratic identity of autonomy within the wider frameworks of the UK and European Union.

The declared values that undergird the Scottish Parliament are *access, fairness and power-sharing.*[22] These represent the core values that any post-modern Scot looks for in any institution, including the Church.

In his essay on *God in Society*, Professor William Storrar comments on the divine comedy that the name of the site for the new parliament is "Holyrood" – meaning the Holy Cross.

He traces the word 'holy' through the Anglo-Saxon word 'halig' meaning 'whole'.[23] He then links that with the Old Testament view of salvation, and suggests that Holyrood is to be a place of 'wholeness and healing for an unhealthy, injured, broken, damaged, ground-down and deprived world'. That is quite a calling for any political institution!

He continues by pointing us beyond politics:

> *This wholeness and healing are only possible... because of Jesus, the holy one of Israel, set apart and anointed for God's holy purposes in the world.*
>
> *The Holy Rood – the Holy Cross – is the place where we see shockingly juxtaposed God's suffering love for humanity with the terminal violence of the powerful against the innocent. It is the* <u>*holy*</u> *place precisely because it is a place of healing for a suffering world.*[24]

There is irony here. In some ways the Scottish parliament may be seen to have distanced itself from the Christian heritage of this land, but the strange irony is that it has affirmed core values that flow from the cross of Christ – 'access' (to God), 'fairness' (equality as children of God) and 'sharing of power' (the self-emptying ministry of God in Christ).

The Holy Rood challenges both Scotland and the Churches.

As we think of the emerging Church around Scotland and listen to various stories of new churches in this new Scotland, we need to ask if they are marked by these elements of the Holy Rood – the Holy Cross:

- Do they offer access to the gospel of Jesus Christ to people formerly excluded by inherited models of church life?
- Do they express models of affirmation and valuing of people who have lived under layers of self-rejection and social put down?

• Do they embody patterns of leadership and ministry that express the kenotic self-emptying love of God in Christ?

The irony is that to be culturally relevant in post-modern Scotland, the Church of Jesus Christ must live closer to the cross.

However, the emerging Church struggles to come into being against an undertow of conservatism – an undertow not only in the Church, but embedded in the Scottish culture and psyche.

A comment about the culture of Scotland from a recent social and political analysis of Scotland, *Anatomy of the New Scotland – Power, Influence and Change*, sums up the challenge facing the Church in Scotland:

Anatomy of the New Scotland... draws a picture of the contest between the establishment forces of cautious, conservative Scotland and those favouring a more radical, democratic path.

> *It is not and never has been an equal struggle: the former has the political parties, civil service, business and most of civic Scotland on its side, but the latter has the visionaries, dreamers and innovators who will change Scotland.*[25]

This is the struggle for all who want to see new churches for a new Scotland – those who will take up their 'Holy Rood' and follow Christ in Scotland today.

To sum up...

We are at a critical moment. The Church is on the move. A new Church is emerging. The Church for Scotland will emerge as we live close to the cross.

Lesslie Newbigin was once asked if he was optimistic or pessimistic about the Church. We agree with his reply, when he said: 'Neither. I believe in the resurrection.'

Chapter Two

Living with Questions – a view from a post-modern parish

A Persistent Question

In over 30 years of ministry, my calling has been to work within the Church of Scotland. Throughout these years I have experienced the recurring frustration of seeing the responsiveness of people to the gospel of Jesus Christ, but their inability to relate to the inherited patterns of the Church of Jesus Christ. The persistent question has been: 'What kind of church will offer access to the gospel for the next generation?' One answer would be: 'not the church as we know it.'

All statistics show a massive disconnection with people under the age of 45. The implications for church membership and church leadership are obvious. The longer-term implications for the influence of Christian values in family life and community leadership for the next generation are even more concerning. Without more Christians being more Christian, our nation becomes less Christian. The evangelisation of Scotland is the issue at stake.

While research among growing congregations in the Church of Scotland indicates that some churches do hold the seeds of renewal of the Church for the future,[26] my growing conviction is that the time has come for the focus of the question to shift from integration to innovation.

The issue is no longer: 'How do we adjust what we have in order to create space for those who are missing?' In answering that question, the pace of change is too slow for the generation of people growing up outside the Church, and the pain of change is often too great for people within it. It is time for new beginnings, for pilot plants and prototypes, pioneering projects that may clear a path for others to follow. It is vital that we begin the conversation from the other end – it is time to 'stop starting with the Church'. There is a 'Church of the churchless' waiting to be called into being.

To put it differently: 'If I were to land in this culture as a missionary, where would I begin?' I am convinced that it is time to allow a new generation to hear the gospel in new ways and to begin to devise new ways of expressing the gospel community for our times.

The issues of culture, Church, mission and ministry are in the melting pot. The way we see the world, the Church and the patterns of leadership needs massive shifts in existing mindsets.

A Personal Perspective

In August 1997, I was appointed associate minister at the parish church of St Cuthbert, in the west end of Edinburgh's City Centre, with a remit to develop appropriate mission strategies for that context. From the outset it was clear that this included developing new patterns of church to relate to a very varied community.

This situation is an example in microcosm of the story of the Church of Scotland. The 1,300 year history of Christian presence on the site of the present St Cuthbert's carries a rich missionary tradition providing the memory banks from which new vision may be fuelled. This 'mother Church' of Edinburgh has given birth to many daughters. However, with a worshipping congregation of 120, of whom 70% are over 60, any hope that this 'Sarah' may give birth again must be rooted in an Abrahamic faith in the God of resurrection!

Field research undertaken between August 1997 and March 1998 revealed the '2,8,20 Parish Profile': 2,000 live in the parish, 8,000 (10,000 by 2003) commute into business daily and 20,000 pass through the parish each weekend in search of entertainment and leisure in theatres, cinemas, pubs and clubs. Most of these commuters are under 45 – the age group significantly absent from most churches in most places most of the time.

Continuing in the personal vein, let me share three biblical passages, whose revelation of God in Christ shaped my practical missionary response to this situation. They offer theological clues to mission in this context.

Theological Pointers

Philippians 2 – Christ's Downward Journey of Grace

It was a Sunday in Advent 1996. I visited St Cuthbert's at the invitation of the minister, knowing that the post of associate was open for consideration. The experience was disturbing. Elders met us at the door dressed in morning suits looking like an undertakers' outing. The entrance foyer felt like a mausoleum. The church was immense and elaborate, built in an Italianate high church style of the late 19th century. It spoke of power and wealth and all the messages that would send a shiver down the spine of any post-modern pilgrim. The music consisted of hymns that I had not sung for years. The pulpit was high and distant. The prospect of engaging in mission to the missing generations from this starting point was remote.

Then came the sermon. The message was about Christ coming from glory to meet us where we are. Linking the kenotic movement of grace in Philippians 2 with Christ's identification with the 'least of these' in Matthew 25, Tom Cuthell, the minister, ended with a startling statement that God's mission was about 'Christ meeting Christ.'

In that moment, I sensed that this grand old dowager

lady of Edinburgh was being called to step down from the place of status and power and assume the role of servant and evangelist in a street level ministry. If that was the call on the congregation, then I believed God was calling me to share in that calling to follow Christ to meet Christ on the street. Together as a congregation we would struggle to respond to that call in the coming years.

Acts 18 – I have many people in this city

By August 1997, I was walking the streets of the parish, sensing total inadequacy for the task. Nothing in my training or experience had equipped me for this exposure to the arrogant business buildings, or the vast crowds on the weekend streets making their way to the clubs or the homeless men sleeping in the graveyard. I suffered from an acute dose of ecclesiastical agoraphobia! I was outside my comfort zones of pulpits, congregational life and the predictability of Kirk Session decision-making.

For weeks I walked and prayed, by day and by night. Then one evening, the word came. From Acts 18 where Paul, the former Jewish Rabbi was experiencing the angst of cross-cultural exposure to the streets of Corinth, came these words of encouragement:

> *Do not be afraid. Keep on speaking and do not be silent. For I am with you. I have many people in this city.*[27]

In that moment I was given the X-ray vision to see in every business, club, theatre and shop, God's 'many people'. My job was to go and find them – those who knew they were his people and those who were his not-yet people.

Strange as it may seem, that passage was to carry within it the seeds of our strategy – where Paul started with the business community of Corinth and ended up outside the synagogue, operating off-site in the 'house next door'. That was to become our strategy too.

Colossians 1 – The Colossal Christ of Colossians

As time passed, the other passage which came to describe my journey and inform my approach was Colossians chapter 1 – read backwards! Paul ends the chapter speaking about 'Christ in you the hope of glory'[28] – that personal presence of Christ within us. That was my faith motivation for many years. Read backwards and we come to Christ as head of his body, the Church – an insight which had freed me from an individualistic faith into a greater recognition of the communal nature of the Church of all ages, nations, cultures and generations.

Walking the streets of the city led me one step further on that journey to recognise that Christ is the head of all things; that all things were made by him, through him, and for him, and that in Christ all things hold together.

These massively comprehensive words helped me to recognise that in the city, all aspects of city life would to find their fulfilment in Christ. There were no exclusion zones.

Post-modernism may be suspicious of the Big Story, but Christians cannot afford to lose confidence in that cosmic view of Christ – not as a totalising power-claim, but as an all-embracing story that offers meaning to a world that gives Oscars to 'the Lord of the Rings' because for a few hours it was invited to be part of a cosmic drama.

Philippians and Colossians offer us two Christologies and two missiologies. As Ray Bakke, the creative writer in Urban Mission, has pointed out: in his Bible Philippians and Colossians sit side by side. The new Church for a new generation will need that bifocal vision to follow this Christ.

The Post-modern Microcosm

Good leadership begins with a 'knack for the here'[29]. Current approaches to practical theology mean that 'it is unthinkable in many churches to engage in any theological reflection without first studying the context in which it is taking place.'[30] The missing generation is not an abstract set of statistics, but real people living in our locality. For this reason we now offer a description of the parish, focussing on the issues and questions it raises. This offers a window on many different lifestyles.

Let me take you on a brief tour of our city centre parish.[31] It is a microcosm of our post-modern culture. It is like visiting an archipelago of islands.

Group 1 – The Residents

Residents are mobile and have little sense of belonging to the neighbourhood. For generations families had lived in the tenements around the area, belonging to interlocking communities including the church. Demolition, decanting and depopulation broke up that community in the 1960s. By the end of the 20th century and the beginning of the 21st century, the residents had long lost that sense of connectedness.

Post-modern people are rootless and mobile. The quest for relationship reaches beyond geographical proximity. They belong to networks around the city; of leisure, sport, work or education.

Issue No. 1: What patterns of church community connect with such a fluid culture? When so much of our church life is designed for settled church in settled community, how do we redesign church for a mobile society?

The area was surveyed by visiting and by phone-calls. Regular communication at Christmas and Easter with parish residents through a community newsletter was appreciated, but evoked little response. Not one of the regular worshippers lived in the parish area. The student population was surveyed and attempts were made to develop a partnership of churches to purchase premises for a student drop-in centre, but the project failed. Involvement with the local community council and the local health centre were the best points of contact. The inherited model of neighbourhood church did not work.

Group 2 – The Businesses

Businesses are packed with the stressed out generation; adrenalin addicts often feeling isolated and stressed. Many of the big businesses are led by workaholics and supported by their victims.

Figures at the time revealed that 100 million working days are lost in the UK through stress. Between 150,000 and 200,000 people receive counselling each year (double the number of 10 years ago!), and the economic cost is £20 billion per year.[32]

A stress management course hosted by a local company highlighted the three main stressors as: personal communication, lack of clarity of roles and excessive demands and targets. The missing generation is facing immense stress in the workplace.

The rising generation are refusing to play the old game. 'Work-life balance' has become the Holy Grail. What is life really about? Do I live to work or work to live?

Issue No. 2: How far do worship, pastoral care, Christian education and mission support and equip people who are shaped and often bruised by their working environment?

Our Oasis ministry to the business community was a vital arena of evangelistic engagement for us.[33] Our response was to meet people where they were and ask three questions: How is your business doing? What are the people issues? If you were doing my job how would you do it?

Lunchtime events were hosted in local businesses on business themes and addressed by professionals in their field. In time, credibility and trust grew and more explicit explorations of the Christian faith were offered in a local hotel at lunchtimes through Business Alpha. Workplace ministry is increasingly coming on to the agenda of many churches as the primary area of engagement.

Group 3 – The Weekenders

These come in to play in the pubs, clubs, theatres, cinemas and eating-places. Here is a strange mixture of carnival and lament. People escape the pressures of work or the poverty of the estate. There is a search for transcendence beyond the mundane and for intimacy beyond the mechanical routine of work. Struggling to plant a church in the club culture of the city has been a major challenge for us.[34]

Jurgen Moltmann's *Theology and Joy* challenges the eschatology that is posited only on a notion of purpose. He asks what is left when the purpose is fulfilled. Only an endless sense of boredom remains. Heaven, by contrast, is an eternity of 'wasted time' in the sense that there is nothing more to be achieved. Instead, the sole focus is worship, 'totally without purpose as a hymn of praise for unending joy, as an ever-varying round dance of the redeemed in the Trinitarian fullness of God, and as the complete harmony of soul and body.'[35]

This joyful eschatology casts a new light on our playful entertainment community. Are the dancing clubbers dancing at the gates of Hell or are they closer to heaven than we realise? Think of the Biblical Festivals and Jesus at parties with friends. What do the gospel stories about eating and drinking have to say about places of eating and drinking as places of community and engagement?

Issue No. 3: How do we celebrate God in the midst of the playfulness of life in the places where people meet to enjoy life? What about cinema as the forum of public theological debate?

In a specially commissioned research video of the nightlife of the parish, the manager of the Revolution night-club spoke of people looking for new patterns of community as regular customers made their way to his club on Fridays and Saturdays.

Tellingly he said that if the Church wanted to be relevant to his clubbers, 'it must become part of the pattern and routine of our lives'. I wondered if he had been reading Incarnational theology! His words have prompted a deep challenge to an ageing church to ask how we might do just that. A decision to engage in a night-club chaplaincy and ultimately to plant a church for that nightclub community raised again the persistent question: 'What kind of church will offer access to the gospel for these people?'

Group 4 – The Homeless

The homeless are the prophetic people on the streets. Without cheapening the harsh reality of those without roof or home, the theme of the homeless nomad has been used as a description of our culture.[36] It may be that, in our dealing with the realities of homeless people, we learn how to become the hospitable place for those who are 'lost at sea without a light or a lighthouse' to guide them.

The spirituality of hospitality lies at the heart of being the Church of Jesus Christ, for it lies at the very heart of God the

Trinity who invites us to share the communion of love: God the Creator who creates space for new worlds to emerge, and God who, in the incarnation of Jesus, empties himself in poverty to make room for us in the generosity of eternal life.[37]

Issue No. 4: How does the Church offer healing hospitality to the most vulnerable of our generation? How do we remain open to hear the voice of the voiceless and be evangelised by the poor?

Our response was to share with a consortium of churches over the winter in offering a meal, bed and breakfast for the worst nights of the year. As we opened our church for people to sleep inside for a few nights in the winter, we saw that they were younger and younger. Six years ago it was the old alcoholics. Today it is the young drug addicts in their 20s. Most of them have lost a home long before they lost their house. They scream at us about the relational deficit at the heart of our society. Families have broken down. Communities of care do not exist. God speaks from the pavements. Where is home for the homeless spirits of our time?

Group 5 – The Shoppers

These represent the first generation to see shopping as entertainment. The consumer mentality puts 'choice' as the idol at the heart of our society. Shop for your furniture or for your spirituality. My right to choose is the core value of post-modernity.

Following the imagery of Zygmunt Baumant's 'liquid modernity' where we have moved from 'heavy capital' fixed in mines and factories to the 'flow' capital of information which travels light in computers, Pete Ward suggests that we need to move from solid church to 'liquid church' that 'connects with the liquid flow of spiritual hunger in our societies.'[38]

Issue No. 5: How do we offer a range of options of times and styles and venues for spiritual exploration to the consumer society?

One response was to offer WWW – Wednesday Worship With... – a monthly evening of reflective worship with music, movement, candlelight and space for reflection. In the middle of the day it offers a place of sanctuary for business people. In the evening it offers a quiet space for those for whom the wordiness of worship is a barrier to hearing the word of God.

Over the Christmas period literally hundreds of people enter city centre churches for a range of services in a range of styles. One neighbour offers a shoppers' service at 4pm on the Sunday before Christmas, while we could welcome 200 people on Hogmanay to bring in the new year.

Sunday by Sunday worship is offered in a distinctive liturgical style with a strong choral tradition. On Sunday evenings there is a service of healing with the anointing of oil and corporate prayer; a small caring community of praying people faithfully available to people who come from miles around in search of God's blessing in their need.

Group 6 – The Surfers

Surfers are the web-linked generation. They are all around us in the internet transfer of investment funds, and the communication technology that is the infrastructure of life. 'The Web' is an icon of interconnectedness. Web-links enable our communication with the businesses in our area and open conversations across the world.

Issue No. 6: Where are the virtual evangelists who speak in the language of cyberspace?

The church website attracted tourists from around the world to visit and to pray on an ancient site of prayer. Our business ministry has grown exponentially since we gained access to the e-mail of all businesses. On the morning after the tragedy of September 11 in New York, businesses opened their e-mails to messages of support from Oasis and the invitation to an open church for prayer and reflection. The ministry among clubbers remains small on the ground, but is 'blogging' across the world among clubbers and Christians looking for fresh expressions of church.

Group 7 – The Asylum Seekers

Asylum seekers remind us that we are part of a global generation. They remind us of the violence of the world in which we are global citizens. The asylum seekers remind us that global connection means global responsibility. Churches around our cities have offered care and welcome for asylum seekers and refugees caught in the trap of endless migration.

Issue No. 7: Where is the Church as advocate that stands alongside and speaks up for those who seek a new home in a strange land?

St Cuthbert's has a long history of international connections. Israel-Palestine, Mozambique, Pakistan, and Kenya have all been in partnership with this city church. Morning and evening worship is often made up of people from several continents travelling from everywhere to everywhere.

For a period we welcomed an Indian priest as part of the church team. He laid down the prophetic challenge that, while we had the connections and the transient visitors, we were yet to become an international congregation at the heart of an international city. Links with the Scots International Church in Rotterdam, their Mamre ministry to refugees and 50% of the church leadership originally from Africa left questions about the racial diversity needed to be a church offering hospitality to the displaced stranger in an international, multicultural city.

Group 8 – The Ageing Congregation

In common with most congregations, this city centre church is growing markedly older with a high proportion of people in their 80s and 90s – among them great saints of God with gifts of humour and character to inspire anyone.

In our focus on the 'next generation', there must be no hint of ageism in the Church of Jesus Christ. In a Scotland where the demographics all point to an increasing number of people over the age of 65 in the population, there are issues about the spiritual nurture and the evangelisation of older people.

Issue No. 8: How do we encourage a spirituality of ageing that is both affirming for those who are part of the Church and attractive for those who are not (yet)?

Ministry to the elderly takes many forms depending on the stages of ageing – from the active involvement of the fit who give time and energy to coffee mornings and home-visiting to the support of those who are less active but can phone or pray or welcome others into their homes. There is also the crucial care of those who have stepped out of this world's traffic through loss of mobility or loss of mental faculties, and the accompaniment on the final journey – the enablement of dying well.

Into this core ministry (replicated around the country in good parish ministry), we introduced a less usual element of care – a course for carers on the spirituality of ageing. This short course helped elders, visitors and carers to recognise the changing patterns of life in old age, and to affirm in them all the image of God to the end.

In relation to our theme of the next generation, we need older people – the Simeons and Annas of our time – boundary people living with a spirituality of waiting for God's promise to come, and who have the discernment to recognise God's new birth when it arrives.

It has been my intention here to focus on one congregation in one city centre community in order to recognise issues that affect many churches across Scotland today. This local community raises vital sociological and theological issues for shaping the Church of the future; issues that may begin to offer access to the gospel for this alienated generation.

The Post-modern Parish

Facing up to these issues has led to the exploration of specific patterns of Christian community for the business and the night-club constituencies to which we will return later.

First, let me comment on the parish principle. Many people see the parish as an outmoded paradigm for mission. That is only partially true. There is a need to hold together the elements of territory, neighbourhood and network. Our inherited approach is to think territorially – and that still holds in some rural communities and small towns. Increasingly, through recognising 'natural communities' and parish groupings, we are working to the contours of neighbourhoods – but more and more, people are finding their identity and community in networks of work, leisure or cyberspace rather than in their local neighbourhood.

Nonetheless, the parish can still offer a starting point for authentic mission. The parish principle requires churches to take responsibility for the people who live in or who move through that neighbourhood. Without that responsibility, would St Cuthbert's have taken the initiative in mission?

However, the post-modern parish is a honeycomb of mini-cultures already inhabited by God's Spirit and God's people and aching to be redeemed into the liberation of God's purposes.

The parish represents a 'circle of accountability' within which a church may take the initiative in mission and evangelism, and where, in humility, we must share in partnerships with others to share in God's mission.

Partnership is essential to the future. In the west end of Edinburgh, two Church of Scotland churches and one Scottish Episcopal church have a long history of collaboration. In recent years their partnership has refocussed on shared initiatives in mission, locally and globally, shared opportunities for worship and Christian nurture, and covenanted commitments to shared decision-making. The ministers and staff of the churches have met on a regular basis for meals, retreats and planning, learning to work together as a team. That grouping is being extended to become a city-centre grouping, mandated to review the mission opportunities of the city centre and to review how the resources of the various churches may be deployed to fulfil that mission.

This view challenges any possessive approach to parish. The parish concept goes sour when the parish becomes a territory marked out as a possession where other missionary spirits are viewed as intruders. The parish potential is vitiated when the area is seen as the fodder to sustain the Church, rather than the field into which the Church is called to sow, plant, serve and harvest. Parish boundaries are as thick or as thin as we want to see them. There are churches which need to be blessed with God's gracious gift of 'boundary blindness'. Together they can then engage in God's mission in their shared ministry area. That is the goal of the new initiatives in area team ministry.

Our word for parish has its origins in the Greek word *paroikos*, meaning 'the stranger who lives alongside'. The parish church may be described as 'a gathering of called out ones who, in the name of Jesus Christ, seek the welfare of the stranger who lives alongside us.'[39]

At the end of the day, it comes down to the age-old issue of law or grace: either the parish is a legal entity to be protected, or a sign of the calling of the Church of Jesus Christ to make known the grace of God in Jesus to every nook and cranny of the nation – in every neighbourhood and every network.

The Theology and Spirituality of Grace

The persistent question about church for the missing generation is more than a pragmatic response to cultural alienation. It is a theological question about how we become a church rooted in the gospel of grace. It is an issue of theology that shapes our core spirituality.

Dominic Smart of Aberdeen recently defined church solely in terms of grace:

> *Church is a group of people brought together by God, knowingly receiving and giving the grace of God, for the glory of God.*[40]

The only definition of grace that we find in the Bible is Paul's description to the Corinthians as he encourages them to be generous:

> *For you know the grace of our Lord Jesus Christ, that though he was rich, yet for your sakes he became poor, so that through his poverty you may become rich.*[41]

That definition is in turn a short-hand version of the magnificent Christological hymn of Philippians 2:5-11 where we are called to share Christ's downward journey of obedience and service and celebrate the upward journey of authority and confidence. Grace is not a theological characteristic attached to an abstract God. Grace is the nature of God revealed in Jesus Christ. We are called to reflect that image as we are changed from glory into glory by the Spirit. It is a church shaped by grace that will be released to be the Church for the next generation.

Grace is a *movement of generosity*. It is the nature of the

God of grace to give, go and send, for his nature is love. The missionary Father sends the missionary Son who releases the missionary Spirit to empower a missionary people to share in God's mission in God's world. The Church that reflects the image of God will live in the grace of God and live out the grace of God. That is the core of our liberation from the mindsets that bind us in structural fundamentalism.

Grace is the *model of ministry and mission* that is shaped by the Incarnation evidenced in Jesus who 'became flesh and lived among us'[42] – or to use the translation of Eugene Peterson in *The Message* – 'the word became a human being and moved into the neighbourhood' – and we would add, 'into the networks'. God takes the initiative and comes alongside us, even inside our skin and saves from within, not from a distance. The Church shaped by grace will do likewise.

Grace *gives up position and power* in order that others may enjoy new status and position. Grace challenges patterns of ministry to be shaped by the mind of the Servant, breaking down the walls of leadership dominance – whatever the name or office attached to that leadership role might be. Grace comes alongside and creates space for the other to 'become rich' and to rise up in Christ to become all that they can become in his resurrection life.

Grace *inspires us to travel* from our familiar, settled centres of church life into uncertain environments beyond our control. The mission of God is an overflow of grace from eternity to eternity. This journey of grace has its impetus in the centrifugal power of the Holy Spirit seen in the Acts of the Apostles crossing cultural and geographical boundaries[43] – from Jerusalem (familiar territory), to Judea (still people like us) to Samaria (taboo territory) and to the ends of the earth (places beyond our imagination). Grace challenges us to find the 'no go areas' of our community and go there! The Church is saved when it is on the road again.[44]

Grace *lies at the heart* of the Church's decision-making to make space for people not like us. In the Council of Jerusalem when the travellers' tales of Paul and Barnabas about the conversion of the gentiles meet the tradition of the Jewish-rooted Church, the decision-making is based on the foundations of grace by Peter:

> *We believe it is through the grace of our Lord Jesus Christ that we are saved, just as they are.*[45]

The result is a foundational principle set down by James:

> *It is my judgement that we are not to make it more difficult for the Gentiles who are turning to God.*[46]

If these were guiding principles of our church's decisions at every level, there would be a quiet revolution. It is the core tradition of the Church to become the Church for the not-yet church.

Grace lies at the heart of the primary biblical motif of the pilgrim people of God who are called to a destination far beyond our current structural definitions of church. The Church of tomorrow is a gift of grace yet to be discovered and defined. The tyranny of precedent is broken when we believe that we have not yet become the Church of the new creation. Grace sets us free to dream of God's glory filling the earth.

We are called to travel with the Spirit towards the horizons of new creation, always an 'interim church' breaking new ground:

> *The Church is essentially en route, on a journey, a pilgrimage. A church which pitches its tents without looking out constantly for new horizons, which does not continually strike camp, is being untrue to its*

calling… It is essentially an interim church, a church in transition, and therefore not a church of fear, but of expectation and hope; a church which is directed towards the consummation of the world by God …[47]

The Church of Jesus Christ is yet to be. May our memories not be a barrier to our imagination.

Chapter Three

Towards the Open Ground – tracing movements for change

Learning a New Language

In terms of missionary engagement, the Church has too often been like the British on the continent, expecting everyone to speak English. As one business man commented, 'That is fine if you want to buy, but not enough if you want to sell.'

We have expected people to understand our language, but we are still slow to learn the language of the emerging culture – be that the technological language of interactive websites and text messaging, the visual language of cinema, the musical language of MTV or the relational language of power-allergies and participative decision-making. At best we have offered people who come to our churches lessons in 'Christendom' and invited them to join our sub-culture.

In fairness, many churches are working hard at expressing the gospel in the language of the modern culture. Community involvement from lunch clubs to credit unions creates authentic connections of care in the community. 57% of church-goers (60% of Church of Scotland church-goers) are involved in community welfare, amounting to 52,000 people or 1% of the population. When midweek activities are included, the Church interacts with another one person for every three in worship, taking the 'contact' level up to 15.1% of the population.[48]

The body language of community and hospitality offers a place of belonging to the 'Friends' generation. Better visual communication and a wider range of music helps to engage the newcomer. The miracle of the simple meal lies at the heart of the evangelising success of Alpha courses across the Western world. Alpha has been used by 1,100 churches in Scotland and involved 46,800 people over the past three years, but it has not yet contributed to growth in the majority of cases.[49]

Cell groups help people to find their gifts and contribute instead of being passive observers. Some larger churches respect the need for a cooler relationship of anonymity and non-involvement.

Congregational renewal

Since congregation is the normative expression of Church life in these islands, much energy goes into congregational renewal for mission.

Our American cousins with their genius for analysis and organisation have given us ways to reshape congregational life with inspiring worship, warm fellowship, deeper discipleship, clearer communication and selfless service. The names of Willowcreek in Chicago and Saddleback in Los Angeles are well known and well respected by many as sources of inspiration.

However, they operate in a church-going Christendom culture that is some 40 years behind us. At its best, their wisdom leads to 'better sameness' which wins back the de-churched, and that is good. At worst, it may lead to disillusionment as models and methods are transposed rather than translated and adapted to our more deeply secularised culture.

Congregational development is almost a growth industry. There are many tools to help assess a congregation's health and develop a more effective pattern of congregational life for our culture and times. The Church of Scotland has offered 'Congregational Mission Design' as a process of developing an overall vision for missional development, while the Scottish Episcopal Church offers 'Mission 21', based on the work of the Alban Institute; rooted in a Trinitarian spirituality of invitation and participation. One area of Scotland is currently working on the German Church Growth Institute's findings in 'Natural Church Development' with its eight key factors for a healthy church.

A few others have picked up on the seven health indicators from 'Building Bridges of Hope' from the Churches Together in Britain and Ireland (CTBI). BBH identified these health indicators in churches which have missional integrity:

1. Focussing Vision
2. Community Partnerships
3. Sharing Faith and Values
4. Nourishing Ordinary Life
5. Developing Shared Leadership
6. Becoming a Learning Congregation
7. Open to being accompanied on the journey

Many of these themes are common to other schemes of analysis, but the three themes which stand out from other grids as pointers to the future are:

nourishing ordinary life: allied to the growing recognition of equipping people for daily life in the workplace;

becoming a learning congregation: not so much about education as the capacity for continuous reflection, refocus and redirection (both personal and corporate);

willingness to be accompanied on the journey: a mixture of the mentor who affirms what God is doing in the congregation and the coach who challenges people to further faith and obedience.

Where the congregational model is still sustainable and appropriate, these processes of reflection and transformation are urgently needed for a comprehensive overhaul of most congregational lives. The danger is of minor tweaking that does not face the pain barrier of fundamental change.

Generational body language

The underlying question throughout this book is: What kind of church will offer access to the gospel for the next generation? None of these congregational development models addresses the issue of generational patterns of belonging and believing which would bring a cultural critique to the assumed starting point of 'congregation' as our template.

Studies in the 'generations' divide those born in the 20th century into cohorts of approximately 20 years, each defined by their year of birth, and the cultural shapers of that 20 year period.

God and the generations – youth, age and the Church today [50] is a report on this theme by the Evangelical Alliance, published in 2002. The editors, David Hilborn and Matt Bird, speak of five generations in the UK:

1. The World War generation (b. 1901-24) – a generation marked by the discovery of flight, medical advances and atomic energy; those who pioneered the space race. For them the world is about finding order, faith is about reason and argument, and church is where all things are done decently and in order.

2. The Builders (b.1925-45) – a generation who lived through the Depression and the Second World War and made their mark by aiming to build a better world in the post-war period. They have a strong sense of civic values, are very pragmatic and ask, 'Does it work?' Church is a place of practical service and duty.

3. The Boomers (b.1946-63) – the post-war generation (which created the 'permissive society') had a more egalitarian view of society, lived more with feelings and looked for faith and church to be more experiential. They were part of the Jesus Movement and the Charismatic Movements of the 1970s and 80s.

4. The GenXers (b.1964-81) – the generation (sometimes called 'busters' because they lived through the 'bust-up' of family life) live with a sense of being let down by society. They live out the 'hermeneutic of suspicion' as a way of life, with a poor ability to trust unless they sense that you are genuine. The key word for them is authenticity. The quest is for relationships.

5. The Mosaics (b.1982 onwards) – the most highly-regulated generation of the century, with signs of returning to being more civic-minded. Faith for this generation is likely to be more individual, but expressed best in a community.

Some key expectations and outlooks of these generational groups are usefully summarised in the report of the Scottish Church Census, *Turning the Tide – The Challenge Ahead.*[51]

The Generations

Ages	**Builders 58-76**	**Boomers 39-57**	**Gen X 20-38**	**Mosaics 1-19**
Respect	Status	Competence	Openness	Involvement
Support	Can manage	Like it	Need it	Mobile use
Work	Happy to do anything	Specialise	Look to team	Own business
Church	Good Habit	Like to use gifts	Attend when feel like it	What's Christianity?
Think...	Linear and logic	Linear and logic	Creatively	Fragments

This table highlights important issues. Firstly, the inherited Church is shaped by the Builders and Boomers. It is assumed that Generation Xers and Mosaics grow up into Builders and Boomers. They do not. The cultural 'fit' is different.

Secondly, we have already noted that the average age of the church member is 47 – rising to 56 years by 2020 – but the lead cohort in society is the 18-38 age group. If they shape society, but find no place in church, the abyss widens and deepens. The key issue is one of power and control. In most churches, culture is controlled by builders and boomers. The response is one of spirituality – the spirituality of grace, creating space for the energy of Generation X and the creativity of Mosaics.

Gary McIntosh[52] simplifies the grid to three generations, builders (59+), boomers (40-58) and busters (21-39) at 2004. This grid is adapted from McIntosh's work.[53]

Builders 59+	Boomers 40-58	Busters 21-39
Commitment to Christ		
= commitment to Church	= commitment to relationships	= commitment to family
Programme Oriented	People-oriented	Community Oriented
Money to missions	Money to people	Money to causes
In-depth Bible Study	Practical Bible Study/share	Issue-based Bible study
Loyalty to denomination	Loyalty to people	Loyalty to family
Minister out of duty	...for personal satisfaction	...to meet needs
Support missions	Support big causes	Support local causes

This table exposes the changing motivations across the generations, especially in relation to financial giving and personal commitment.

It is hardly surprising that one minister summarised the position of the Church of Scotland as being 'two generations adrift.'[54] We might add – 'and still drifting!'

Inventing a new language

Returning for a moment to our analogy of learning a new language, we might draw a comparison from the Caribbean where colonists spoke English and expected others to do likewise. Later, English and local dialects blended to form 'pidgin English'. Many of our churches are moving to that stage of cultural engagement where the language (and body language) of church is starting to blend with the culture of surrounding society.

However, the next stage of linguistic development in the Caribbean led to the emergence of 'Creole', which bore little resemblance to either of its languages of origin. The shifts in our culture are more substantial than we have recognised and the patterns of church which we need demand the development of 'Creole Church'. We are now beyond learning new a language. We are at the stage of having to invent a new one which will resonate within our culture. In the words of Brian McLaren, it is time to 'maximise discontinuity'[55] as we grapple with where church and culture are at today.

Leonard Sweet used the imagery of the tidal wave (tsunami) to express the extent of the changes we are experiencing in this post-modern phase of history. He defines this as a 40 year transitional phase; from an 'Information Age to a Bionomic Age which will begin no later than 2020':[56]

> *We have moved from the solid ground of* terra firma *to the tossing seas of* terra aqua. *The Dick-and-Jane world of my 50's childhood is over, washed away by a tsunami of change... While the world is rethinking its entire cultural formation, it is time to find new ways of being the Church that are true to our post-modern context. It is time for a Post-modern Reformation.*[57]

In his *Post-modern Pilgrims*[58], Sweet argues for the formation of EPIC churches – EPIC being an acronym for Experiential, Participatory, Image-Driven and Communal-Connected to life. He also suggests that:

> *The institutional Church in the next twenty years will continue more and more to look like the pink cadillac with the large tail fins.*[59]

He pleads for the communication of an 'ancient future faith'[60] that is rooted in scripture but translated into culture, not so much through well-prepared sermons, but through offering a total experience.[61] He invites us to become participatory communities where storytelling offers 'fascination, explanation and integration'.[62] In our 'visualholic culture',[63] he speaks of the power of metaphor to bring transformation through capturing the imagination.

In a world of 'connexity' where the Internet is the new public space,[64] he pleads for a new quality of community life where truth is once again related to 'troth' as 'trustworthy truth in relationship'. This is the covenanted commitment which Jesus expected of his disciples, to 'love one another as I have loved you.'[65] Sweet calls this 'The Titanium Rule', several degrees stronger than the so-called golden rule to 'love your neighbour as yourself'.[66]

Where might we look in the Scottish Church scene for any attempts at this radical translation of gospel community for the emerging culture? Three movements within the Church of Scotland may be pointers in this direction, and each has its own acronym: Church Without Walls (CWW), Urban Priority Areas (UPA) and New Charge Development (NCD). This is not to ignore other movements in other areas of Scottish church life, but these are the ones of which I have some personal knowledge and involvement.

Church Without Walls

The most important outcome of the report of the Special Commission anent Review and Reform to the General Assembly of 2001 may be its title *Church Without Walls* – a metaphor of movement, travelling light, connection to our community, and removing the obstacles of unnecessary divisions within and between our churches.

CWW's true simplicity lies beyond that; in focussing on the words of Jesus which started it all: 'Follow me.' These two words determine the purpose of the Church, the shape of the Church and a process of continuing reform for the Church – fulfilling the threefold remit of the Special Commission.

The command to 'follow me' even meets Sweet's EPIC criteria for 21st century post-modern church: offering experiences of going to people and places of Jesus' choosing – beyond our comfort zones; providing lots of opportunity for participation in meals, service and conversation; learning the power of the image from the master of metaphor and story, while learning the meaning of being connected as a community, bound together by the ultimate truth of a crucified and risen Lord.

Two other key words in the report are 'local and relational', inviting the Church to undergo a relational reformation. The Church is stripped back to the bare essentials of four shapers:

1. The gospel – encouraging congregations to let Matthew, Mark, Luke and John be pastors of the congregation for a year, tutoring them in their distinctive patterns of discipleship;

2. The locality – taking seriously the place where the Church is set in city centre or island, in rural glen or expanding town, but looking deeper into the patterns of life that are actually there, and looking more widely to the cultural changes that are affecting us;

3. Friendship – seeing the quality of Christ-informed relationships as the ultimate gift to a world that has lost the art of friendship;

4. Gifts – letting the Church be re-grouped around the gifts and passions of people, supporting them in their everyday callings, rather than de-skilling people by asking them to support church structures.

The CWW movement saw that the challenge would not be to change external structures, but to change internal mindsets:

• From Church focus to Christ focus
following Jesus to see what Church forms round him

- From settled Church to Church as a movement
going where people are rather than waiting
for people to come
- From a culture of guilt to a culture of grace
freeing people to risk and fail
- From running congregations to building communities
working towards a relational reformation
- From isolation to interdependence
encouraging churches to work together
- From individualism to teamwork
seeing teamwork as essential to all ministry
- From top down Church to upside down Church
putting the local church at the centre of the agenda
- From centralised resources to development resources
releasing funds to encourage local vision
- From faith as security to faith as risk
looking for new courage to break out of old routines

In terms of the generational divide, the report recognised that a two-pronged strategy was required:

o Urging congregations to determine to integrate children and young people into the life of the congregation; and

o Offering the resources to plant a church for a new generation alongside the current congregation.

The report makes a passionate plea for children and young people to be welcomed into a community of grace and acceptance. We quote it in full:

> *We are a covenant community. By baptism we welcome children into that covenant community, but too often our congregations fail to be the covenanting community needed for children and families to flourish in faith and life. ... Community is built on names. The friendships will begin when every member can name some of the children in the Sunday School or*

the youth club.

Young people are crying out for the Church to recover the relational quality and integrity characterised by the grace and truth of Jesus. In the 'Friends' generation, young people are finding new places of community and belonging. The church culture of formality, regulations, expectations and conformity sends out a corporate 'vibe' that makes today's generation instinctively uncomfortable.

A church that can trace 40 years of declining youth statistics must ask if all the excellent youth work of two generations has been frozen out of church life because we have failed to build relationships of friendship across the generations. We have been caught in the mythology of the generation gap instead of being pioneering myth busters.

Communication with the next generation will require many creative youth ministry skills and pioneering work to develop new patterns of church, but communication without community will be sterile. Every person brings gifts to the community that create the space for young people to feel they belong and that they matter. With Jean Vanier we celebrate the 'gift of the grandmother' in building community.

According to the French sociologist, Danielle Leger Hervieulle,[67] faith is communicated through the generations through the 'chain of memory' in the shared stories, rituals and common life of the faith community. In Western Europe, the 'chain of memory' has been broken. Our challenge is to forge a new chain with the next generation, beginning from the crèche up with our children and grandchildren, nurturing them in the covenant communities of family and Church.

However, CWW also recognised that as the opportunity for integration diminishes, the time comes upon us to plant new churches alongside the old for a new generation. That is our primary theme.

Urban Priority Areas

One place where the Church has had to face the need for radical reshaping has been in the Urban Priority Areas. Here the next generation is marked by the limitations of poverty, family disintegration, physical and emotional abuse, addictions to alcohol and drugs, and a vortex of despair that either crushes the human spirit or calls out extraordinary faith, compassion and courage.

Much has been done in recent years to assess the challenges of being a gospel community in these areas of poverty, both theologically and practically. If we are to think of church for the next generation, we must face the uncomfortable fact that the gap between church and the emerging generation is greatest in these areas of social need. As an insight into how the Church in UPAs is rising to the challenge we will draw on one particularly creative piece of research.

When the World Council of Churches asked for a Scottish response to its paper (nr. 181) on *The Nature and Purpose of the Church* (1999), the Church of Scotland took the creative step of inviting the Panel on Doctrine to take this densely theological treatise, and test its validity by visiting a number of projects under the aegis of the Priority Areas Fund (now the Scottish Churches' Community Trust) which supported work in areas of social need.

These projects included:

• the West End Churches' Key Fund in Glasgow helping homeless people find that first deposit for renting a flat

• the Abigail Project in Possilpark supporting families of young drug addicts

• the Star Project in Paisley where two Church of Scotland churches support a community flat working with two Roman Catholic sisters

• the Colston Milton Drama Project working with Church of Scotland, the Methodist Church and the local community

• the Ripple Project based in St Margaret's in Restalrig and Lochend, Edinburgh, offering information, listening and referral in the community

Out of the dialogue between the WCC document and these local projects, themes were identified that mark out patterns of emerging church:

Community
Advocacy
Spirituality
Hospitality
Service
Proclamation and
Openness to change

The new theme is *advocacy* – a prophetic feature significantly absent from most of the other descriptors of emerging church. This is the point where compassion must be mixed with a strong dose of courage.

Commenting on the University of Glasgow's report on the Church as Social Capital, Dr John Flint, one of the researchers and authors of the report, noted that while the Church was strong on community involvement, we still backed off from political action that might upset the 'powers that be'. We have more to learn about socio-political advocacy as a Church. For a generation with a keen sense of the injustices of the world, there are many who will stand with the Church or against it on the basis of our position on socio-political concerns.

The other theme of the report is *ecumenical partnership.* Observing the significance of these projects as expressions of God's love in the community, the report comments:

> *If it is possible to visit a local church, at worship*
> *or in its other gatherings, and identify with certainty*

the denomination to which it belongs, then perhaps we have spent too much time and energy conforming and not enough in finding the appropriate form that a worshipping, witnessing and serving community needs to take in that place.

The challenge to the Church is, while holding firm to the gospel, to be open to taking the form appropriate to the situation (in which it finds itself).[68]

These words are significant both practically and theologically: at the practical level, it was one of the criteria of the Priority Areas Fund that projects would be ecumenical; at the theological level, they describe the Church that emerges when the key motivation is missionary. The emergence of the Church follows the *Missio Dei.* The Church that takes its identity from that missionary and eschatological perspective will be increasingly ecumenical, moving towards Christ in whom all things are to be reconciled.

Our identities are shaped over-much by our history. In simple terms churches that only look backward and inward will be determinedly denominational. Churches that look forward and outward will be increasingly ecumenical. New churches are to be signs of the new creation.

Anyone who wants to see the grace of God touch every nook and cranny of our nation for the glory of Christ must face the reality that the task cannot be done by one church alone. We need to recover a national vision to see our nation gathered into Christ. Only when the missionary task before us is compelling and overwhelming will our divisions become frustrating enough to require radical reorganisation. The call to unity will be expressed and embraced, not first in the councils of the Church, but in the 'open ground' of God's mission:

The challenge to the Church is to move out into the open ground. There it may find the tools for its own reshaping, so that God's renewing Spirit which continually works through the word, the water, the wine and the bread, through prayer, praise and peace, may not encounter the obstacles of rigidity, lethargy and fear.

We need to be receptive to the voice of God powerfully addressing us from the open ground. Furthermore, we hear best as we venture out, not on errands we ourselves have invented, but responding in love to 'Christ in the stranger's guise'.[69]

As increasing numbers of the population lose historic connections with the denominations, we face a double movement: on the one hand the sour sectarianism of secularised religiosity; and on the other a post-denominational secular ecumenism. For the one group ecumenical partnership is a prophetic sign against destructive social divisiveness; for the other, ecumenical partnership is a pastoral sign of open hospitality to diverse seekers after God.

New Charge Development

Since July 2003, I have been working with the Board of National Mission to support the development of new churches that are being planted under the designation of New Charge Development. While there are many areas of innovation and experimentation across the Church in terms of Congregational Mission Development, Ecumenical Partnerships, Area Team Ministries and imaginative Mission Projects, this is the official 'research and development area' of the Church of Scotland.

NCD is where the Church offers space to experiment, with the freedom to get things wrong before we get them right, with the desire to see churches planted in our culture which have within them from the outset the DNA of a 'missional community', rooted in the gospel and planted in contemporary culture.

There are twelve New Charges: three are on greenfield sites where there is new housing and the opportunity of a new beginning along with an emerging community; four are parish plants from an existing congregation, but with the freedom to develop their own ethos and style, while the remaining five are in parishes where former congregations had come to the end of their life and were legally 'dissolved' to create space for a fresh start.

One these is the *first non-territorial church* in the Church of Scotland, working in partnership with eight other churches of various hues to create a 'new generation' church, beginning with children and young people and working from the ground up for that generational segment under 35. This is based on the recognition that for almost 50 years (since 1957) church youth statistics have been in constant decline, despite excellent youth work around the community.

Only a small proportion has ever integrated into the life of the Church as it is. It seems that with cultural distance being measurable in 20 year cohorts, it is increasingly difficult to 'tilt' the culture of inherited church to make adequate space for the rising generation. What is needed is a parallel church which begins where they are and is then part of a wider network of churches, thus avoiding isolation. This is the first example of network church – 'new alongside old' – in mutual partnership.

Each new charge is unique. One has developed a very distinctive style of *contemporary worship* and creative communication across the age groups in a suburban community, achieving critical mass for continuing growth already. Worship is the dynamic of that church and all else flows from that vision of God. In four years the congregation has grown from 120 to almost 300 people of all ages.

One arose out of moving a church from the city centre to the city edge, with only 40 of the 700 strong congregation opting to form the new missional community (others dispersed to other churches in the city). Driven by the inadequacy of the church to create a supportive community around a young drug addict (who committed suicide), the minister soaked himself in the story of Jesus in Luke and Acts and asked why his church was not following Jesus like that. His theology of Church is to be a 'wounded incarnate community'. *Incarnational mission is the primary dynamic.*

Another grew out of a parish profile. In one particular area of this parish, no resident would come to the church building because of the perceived social divide across a main road. A small fellowship was planted on *the 'cell-church' model* and has now grown in depth and numbers over the past eight years to around 50 committed people. Relational evangelism is at the heart of that church's vision. Youth cells and a youth mentoring scheme offer contact with the new generation. They are already considering how they might move to 'critical mass' and plant a second church from their limited resources to match their unlimited vision. Recent worship offered four optional streams including a workshop on creative writing. They saw numbers rise from 50 to 70.

Some have church buildings and others have chosen to use community centres, schools, health clubs, shop fronts, business centres and other *'proxy places'* with which people already identify themselves. They aim to see the Kingdom grow in the cracks of the community; sustaining a holistic vision of being a community of faith in, of and for the wider community. They avoid the sacred-secular divide which runs through so much church thinking and practice.

Most have a strong focus on *discipleship and spiritual formation* of people in community. There has to be a focus on depth with the few before God can go wide to the many. Too often we strike out to spread the branches wide but there is no root depth to sustain the plant in the wind.

Most new charges are operating in a designated parish setting, but some are *pioneering new partnerships* of cooperation, as former church fellowships are invited to start again as one unit with a fresh missionary vision. Others are working in creative and sacrificial partnership with other parishes in that part of town to operate as a team in ministry and mission.

New charges are marked by a definite *intentionality:* intentionally missional rather than settled; intentionally relational rather than formal; and intentionally spiritual rather than institutional.

New charges are *shaped theologically* by:
the *Missio Dei* – where Church is formed in the slipstream of God's initiating grace;
the *Incarnation* – seeking to culturally appropriate to the community and the wider culture, both connecting and transforming
the *Trinity* – having a high priority on being a relational Church
the *Cross* – being a sacrificial Church in terms of service and the call to discipleship
the *Resurrection* – expecting and experiencing the Risen Christ in the midst
the *Body of Christ* – every person is gifted by the grace of God
the *Holy Spirit* – waiting for God to act and aiming to move in step with the Spirit
the *Grace of God* – aware of being fragile and held by God and ready to be 'given away' by God

New charges are strong on *community engagement and creative relational evangelism*. Worship is marked by celebration, participation and creativity. Spirituality and discipleship are at the core of all programmes helping people to go deeper with

Christ and find their calling in the wider mission of God.

Leaders tend to be catalytic innovators, and the leadership bodies are appointed as people bring a gift to a task for time. There is an inbuilt habit of review; refocus and redirection which operates as continuous *spiral of reflection* and keeps them 'new' in the sense of 'having a fresh focus' on God's future plans.

New charges are pioneering situations which have had some sad *casualties of stress and illness* among their ministers. This arises out of living with the constant experience of 'liminality'[70], living on the borderlands between the inherited Church and the emerging Church. (The prospect of the clean sheet of paper may seem attractive until you have to write on it!)

The massive pressures from competing expectations – the hope of limitless possibilities, and expectations arising from their own passion for the gospel – are just some of the pressures that haunt ministers, either generated by the parent institution or arising from within their own heads. Some of these leaders tend to be almost obsessive and thrive on the chaos, but have to be saved from themselves.

New charges have thrown up important lessons which have relevance for the wider Church:

*1. **Teamwork is vital.*** The new policy is to avoid placing a person in a new charge alone. This pattern of team ministry is being explored elsewhere in the development of area team ministries, and may be one of the major shifts in ethos for the future from the individual minister to the ministry team.

*2. **Support systems are essential.*** A mission developments' facilitator has been appointed for pastoral support. Local new charge commissions have been developed to offer local support. This has been described as 'Rolls Royce' pastoral provision. This should not be a signal to dilute support, but rather to increase it elsewhere as the pressures of missional ministry spread across the Church and more people feel vulnerable in a time of transition.

*3. **Regular review is helpful.*** Each new charge is visited every three years by a team of four for a weekend to reflect together on the current situation and clarify goals for the future. These reviews can be tough, but they act as a catalyst to fresh initiative and are done in a supportive spirit of care for the development of the charge and the people in it. Much of our church life lacks this kind of kindly accountability and so situations drift. This would be a welcome feature of the emerging Church.

4. Ongoing mutual learning is essential. Recognising the gap between the training for ministerial formation and the sharp missionary challenges of church planting (and where is church planting on the training agenda?), ministers and their teams are forming an informal learning network, meeting three or four times a year over a two year cycle for spiritual formation, skills training and theological and strategic conversation. Such a system could be devised among any area based group of ministers or church workers with a minimum of work by a facilitator, calling on the expertise of our theologians to come and engage with our issues on the ground.

A call beyond...

The call of God in the emerging generation is to go beyond where we have come.

1. Beyond activism to the place of stillness and mystery. In our concern for a reorientation of a disconnected church towards God's world in mission, there is a danger that we introduce a level of frenetic activity adding to the workaholic haze of modern life for many people.

Busy people are looking for sanctuary and stillness. The well-documented quest for spirituality which is by-passing the local church, is a search for peace amid pressure, and a service of stillness amid the noise and hurry of life. Where is the discipline of the Sabbath principle – the balance of being and doing, the counter-cultural call to offer a 'pausing place' in a task driven culture? Where is the faith that stops and celebrates the God who keeps the earth turning on its axis and the grass growing in its season without our help?

A well-crafted space, a candle, an image, a few stones or flowers or pieces of wood, a quiet piece of music, a verse of scripture on which to meditate, a gospel story to capture the imagination, time to be still and to know that God is God. That is a gift not to be missed from our activist analyses.

2. Beyond congregation to networks. While many churches are developing the key dynamics of Church for the 21st century, there is another attribute of church – beyond the congregational model – that has begun to be addressed by our 'new generation church'. That is the need for network churches to touch those areas of our segmented culture possibly filtered out by the inherited neighbourhood parish church.

3. Beyond pidgin to Creole. If we are to learn the many languages of our culture, and begin to move from English through Pidgin English to 'Creole Church', then much of that will happen beyond the inclusive neighbourhood church. It will happen by intentional incarnation through the network church which (to pick up our other metaphors) will be flexible enough to surf the waves of cultural change and meet God in the open ground.

4. Beyond the beach to the river. The title of the Scottish Church Census is *Turning the Tide – the Challenge ahead.* The title of this report is misleading to the point of being dangerous. *Turning the Tide* leaves us feeling powerless, for no-one can turn tides. More significantly, it suggests that if we stand at the same point on the beach for long enough, the tide will come back in and lap at our feet. That is an illusion.

A more appropriate metaphor is of a river which has changed its course. The river of the Spirit is running in new places in our culture, and the old patterns of church are being by-passed. Our task is to discern where the river of God is running and form new patterns of church there. That is the missionary call. The Spirit is calling us off the beach to the riverbank.

Ask the youth workers about their sports ministries, the music of youth culture, the search for alternative therapies, the quest for transcendence and intimacy in the nightclubs.

Listen to the women crying out for a spirituality that makes a difference to their lives and the world in which their children are growing up. They are not interested in churches where nothing changes and which change nothing.

Who is coming alongside the men who make little sense of most of what we do?

The tide is not for turning. Is the Church ready to turn and take a long walk to the river?

Chapter Four

Network Church: beginning where people are... and staying there!

Speaking to the moon

A contemporary American writer has said, with his tongue firmly in his cheek, that the first language to be spoken on the moon was English, but it was not somebody from England who spoke it. It was somebody from the colonies! [71]

Let me translate that into our context for you. Most of the people of Scotland who are alienated from the Church as we know it will not hear the gospel through the Church as we know it. They will hear from little colonies of Christian community among the networks of everyday life.

I believe that, in order to engage with the people of the new Scotland, we will be required to invest as much in 'network church' as we have traditionally invested in 'neighbourhood church'.

Stumbling on 'network church'

'Network church' was for me a reality on the ground first before it was a concept. In a sense we stumbled on it in our city centre work in St Cuthbert's, Edinburgh.

St Cuthbert's is a city centre congregation gathered from all over Edinburgh, but nobody living in our parish worships there (see chapter 3). A survey of the neighbourhood (parish) reveals a '2, 10, 20 profile' – 2,000 live there, 10,000 work there and 20,000 come into the area at the weekend for entertainment. Here is a church that lives like an island in the river that flows past its doors, but seldom enters it.

The assumed model of church is the 'suction model',

drawing people through our doors to join us where we are. The challenge was to develop a 'slipstream model', sharing in the mission of God in the community and daring to believe that a different kind of church would form in the slipstream of that movement of grace and self-giving.

In the imagery of the gospels, the Church is simply people with Jesus at the centre, travelling where Jesus takes them. The Church is a movement meeting people where they are in response to the two words of Jesus, 'Follow me'. That simple dynamic lies at the heart of the liberating metaphor of a 'church without walls'.

At best we have operated on a model of gathering and scattering the people of God as individuals. We are now at a time when we need to think about 'dispersed' church as communities of God's people around a central hub.

Every community is a community of communities, a network of networks. For St Cuthbert's, one network in the 'flow cultures' of the city was the *clubbing scene.* God has people in every sector of society, but many of them cannot fit into church as we know it. One clubber describes inherited church as 'one solo person dominating the community space' – a vibe that alienates a subculture in search of participative community. If this group were to be touched by the gospel, it must be by an act of sheer grace – of giving out with zero expectation of people returning to share our church activity. It would need to be a patient planting of a small Christian community that would be in, of and for that cultural group. The new initiative must go. It need not return. Here is grace that offers space for God to create something new.

Friends met in a café. Worship gatherings were held in pubs. Networks emerged to support individuals as they struggled to follow Jesus in this urban culture. The network became international. These networks blended into other networks of care for asylum seekers, of work amidst disadvantaged young people, of hosting 200 people in one week of 24/7 prayer, of finding worship in the dance culture of the clubs. In time ***Raven*** was born as a church for the club scene. In three years we have moved from 'Jerusalem to Antioch' to become the colony from which to reach the moon!

The other obvious set of networks was in the *business community.* The ministry is called ***Oasis*** – originally based on the 'suction model' of inviting people into the church as an oasis of peace in a pressurised world. That made little impact, but people valued the personal connections and visits.

Over a period of ten years, the chaplaincy and church model has evolved into a network church for the business community. All the components of church are there: pastoral care, teaching that integrates life and spirituality, corporate links between the wealth creators and homeless charities, prayer networks, a Business Alpha course to explore the Christian faith, and only recently regular worship opportunities. Everything except the worship happens off-site – in businesses or hotels or restaurants – a network church in, of and for the business community, in turn networked to other churches.

This network strategy extends to the other city centre churches. In response to a Vision and Plan for the City of Edinburgh, they formed a *City Forum* to engage with some of the issues of city life as they affect city policy. The idea was to be better informed so that we could engage in constructive dialogue. The City Forum began a process of surveying the city centre to assess both aspects of city life we cherish and would want to protect, and those aspects of concern which we would want to challenge. Then the city centre churches were grouped together into a formal 'parish grouping'. Over a five year period, this group of churches is mandated to survey the city centre and establish among themselves a 'network of networks' with a mission to penetrate the various networks of the city centre – business, retailers, shoppers, leisure, residents, vulnerable people, decision-makers to name a few.

These examples of network church are not rocket science. Parallel instances can be found around the country where churches are learning to meet people where they are, and allow the relational dynamics of loving God and loving neighbour in the name of Jesus Christ to be recognised as genuine expressions of the Church of Jesus Christ.

The key issue is that we should not see these network contacts as stepping stones to the 'real Church'. They are examples of the emerging Church. The Church is a 'landing craft rather than an ark'.[72] In normal evangelistic work, we go out from the church into the world and come back with others into the Church as we know it. This is not evangelistic work. This is apostolic work. It means that we go out and do not expect to come back. We go where people are... and stay there till church forms there.

Jeremiah spoke of the God who would 'uproot and tear down... build and plant' through the experience of exile.[73] That prophetic word invites us to see the hand of God in the current collapse of inherited patterns of church, and even to see in it the hand of demolition. At the same time we dare to believe that God is building and planting something new for a new generation and a new culture. The God of history is not fazed by this phase of cultural transition.

When we move to the prophecy of Isaiah, we discover God speaking in 'parallel' time. In Isaiah 28, we read of the collapse of Jerusalem, but before the chapter ends, God declares: 'See I lay a foundation stone in Zion ...'[74] Even as the old order falls, the new order is being brought into being. It takes the eyes of the prophet to see it.

The practical issue for the Church in Scotland is whether we see the emerging Church as the sign of God's new order, or some maverick anomaly that veers from the inherited norm. In practical terms that will affect how we train leadership for the future and where we invest our money – to shore up the old or to nurture the new. Do we believe in resurrection, or will we settle for resuscitation?

The Church beyond the congregation

We may be moving into a time when our primary missional model of church will be 'post-congregational'. The word 'congregation' carries with it certain mental models and deeply embedded assumptions about place, people, style, activity. 'Network' is one metaphor to loose the moorings of imagination to discover new possibilities. Network church is one expression of 'the church beyond the congregation'.

The theology of such a possibility needs no justification for those who accept that we are called to share in the 'mission of God'; that the Church is formed as we share as the pilgrim people of God in that movement – to the ends of the earth and the end of time.[75]

The recent report from the Church of England called *Mission Shaped Church*[76], offers a working definition of church-planting which captures the spirit of the network church:

> *Church planting is creating communities of Christian faith as part of the mission of God, to express his Kingdom in every geographical and cultural context.*[77]
>
> *The task is to become church for them, among them and with them, and under the Spirit of God to lead them to become church in their own culture.*[78]

Theologically the report locates its motivation in the mission of God:

> *It is not the Church of God which has a mission in the world, but the God of mission who has a Church in the world.*[79]

And then it makes this vivid shift of focus:

> *Start with the Church and the mission will probably get lost. Start with the mission and it is likely that the Church will be found.*[80]

We turn now to the work of Australian theologian James Thwaites and his provocatively titled book: *The Church beyond the Congregation*.[81]

His thesis is that Western theology and ecclesiology have been affected by Greek dualism that divides spirit/body and sacred/secular. This has led to an overemphasis on the congregational gathering point as the focus of our time and energy. He calls for a Hebrew view of life where we are released from inherited mindsets into a 're-evaluation of our present congregation-focussed approach to church life'.

Thwaites traces that split through Plato, Aquinas, the rationalism of the Reformation and on through the Enlightenment and the Age of Reason. He then identifies how we embody the split in our buildings.

He points out that the early Church had no church buildings until Constantine used pagan temples as the base for Christianity as the imperial religion. Today, buildings are a handicap.

> *In a post-modern time it is becoming more and more obvious that the Christian's split universe, mostly expressed in and from a building we have named church, is benefiting the saints less and less. It is not attracting the attention of the unchurched tribes, heading into the diverse and desperate post-modern mosaic of the 21st century.*
>
> *I believe that our focus for divine meaning and mission on the church gathered is a major strategic error on the part of the Christian Church. It must be overcome if we, as the body of Christ, are to enter into and impact a post-modern world. The Greek split has triumphed by detaching the Church from most of the saints' life and work in creation. The reality we face at this time is that a kingdom divided cannot stand, a people divided cannot act, so a church divided cannot build.*[82]

We heal this split universe by listening to the voice of the Spirit in Creation. The Church finds its identity when we hear that cry and are released to answer its cry. The world will know the Church when the cry it makes is engaged and answered by the people of God.

Unfortunately, 'we continue to listen mostly to our own voices echoing off the walls, defining and redefining us again and again. And we are left wondering why the people don't come'.[83]

> *It is time to look again and locate the new people in Christ that make up the Church. It is time to release them from their church containment set in place by the Greeks and send them into God's creation that, to this day, still knows and calls their name.*[84]

That radical description of the way the Church of the future will be called into being challenges many of our inherited assumptions.

Pass any church building and ask where the church that meets in that building might be on Tuesday morning – at home, in shops, in schools, in hospitals, driving buses, making business deals, typing accounts and so on and so on.

Ask how many networks of people they connect with through the day. How do the arenas of the created order call us to express our faith in ways that inform our lives and transform our society?

For some the nurturing community that meets in that building and in satellite home groups may be sufficient to help them integrate faith and life in a healthy spirituality, living the whole of life in the presence of God revealed in Jesus Christ.

However, for many people there is an uncomfortable sense of 'double isolation' as work and worship take place in different compartments of life. Young mothers, already feeling inadequate to the task of bringing up small children, are made to feel even guiltier about attending church with a noisy child, or not attending because the child is not happy. One new venture in Edinburgh for 20 and 30 somethings has begun a 'motherhood and theology' group to help mothers integrate their faith in to this stage of life. More immediately, a young minister working among youth in schools feels the strain of alienation in the Church's expectations and the contrasting lifestyles of the youngsters.

One of the most challenging scenarios will be in Glasgow, where the City Council has signed up to welcome 6,000 asylum seekers per annum for the next fifteen to twenty years. That will raise many issues of multicultural integration and hospitality, but also issues of ethnic churches such as we have already with Chinese, Asian, Iranian and African churches around the cities.

There is an increasing call for the network church that can meet people where they are ... and stay there!

Let me recommend to you the film 'The Shipping News' with Kevin Spacey and Judi Dench – the wonderful story of a deeply damaged young man named Quoyle who finds freedom and dignity in a fishing village on the coast of Newfoundland.

The metaphor for his life is the house where he stays. It is an old house anchored to the ground by great steel hawsers which strain and howl in the wind.

The book behind the film describes the connection between Quoyle and the house: 'In the house he felt he was inside a tethered animal, dumb but feeling, swallowed by the shouting past.'[85]

That describes much of church life: 'a tethered animal, swallowed by the shouting past.'

The film ends with a great storm in which the house is blown away, but they are left with a view of the sea that they have never had before – a symbol of the new freedom that Quoyle has found.

God is calling us into a new freedom – with a new view of the world in its wonderful interconnectedness – a network of networks within which we live and move and have our being – and where we are to express church in new ways.

All this has great implications for ministry in our times. Thwaites asks for the recovery of the 'apostolic' calling – the calling to lay foundations where no others have laid them:

> *At this time it is the apostolic gift God placed first in the Church that must set the character for all other ministry gifts. Apostolic pastors, prophets, evangelists and teachers must at this time release apostolic saints to break ground and lay hold of their own unique, diverse and rich land.*[86]

That is a challenge for any church to identify those for who are more at home on the edges than at the centre of church, and to release them to be the Body of Christ in the world. Where are the apostolic boundary breakers who must not be contained within church as we know it? We often speak of people who think 'out of the box'. The fallacy is that there is a 'box' to think out of! We need to identify people who already 'live' outside our box and then release and empower them to be church in their sector of the world with whatever network allows them to express Christ where they are.

That is a challenge to all who are called to any form of ministry in these times of missionary challenge and opportunity. It certainly challenges the process of ministerial formation for such a calling.

The Tomorrow Project

Let me introduce now the work Michael Moynagh of the *Tomorrow Project*, which for two years acted as UK think tank on the shape of the Church in 2020, based on interviews and two-day consultations with 200 experts in a range of disciplines from medicine to politics. The findings were distributed to 50,000 decision-makers in May 2000 and the implications for the Church in the UK have been written in the book *Changing World – Changing Church*[87]

The thesis

The thesis of the book is that, based on scenarios of 2020 through the 'Tomorrow Project', the Church will require to offer customised church on a personalised scale, meeting people where they are and forming community where they are. In particular he sees the need to relate to the trends of consumer choice and the world of work in our society.

After reflecting on the decline of the Church in Europe, USA and Australia, he concludes that we need new ways of being church based on the findings of the *Tomorrow Project.*[88]

> *Nothing less than a makeover will equip the Church to reach the changing world that is emerging so rapidly before our eyes.*[89]

Moynagh offers some fascinating images of the Church of the future. For our purposes we will select a few that point specifically to the emergence of 'network church'.

The Church as fellow traveller

We are experiencing a 'radical de-faithing of British society' with 77% of 18 year olds saying they have no religious beliefs (MORI, 1999).[90] The core reason is that we are disconnected from the workplace where people spend most of their time, the consumer who expects a range of choice and high standards of service, and the networks of interest (leisure and sport) where people meet 'people like me'.

On the other hand, we are entering a stage of openness

because people know too little to be hostile, and may be more open and tolerant, especially if we can meet people on their spiritual quest, as suggested by David Hay and Kate Hunt in their research into contemporary spirituality:

> *Spirituality has not been snuffed out by consumerism: rather it may have been heightened as the treadmill of 'spend, spend, spend' leaves people feeling empty inside.*[91]

The Church as connected fragments

When the Church focuses on its core role of being a community of God's people, it can meet people where they are and let new community emerge among the dance culture, among young people after school, in ASDA, among immigrants and among lonely older people. We need a nimble church to engage in a period of experimentation.[92]

In the UK the scenario for 2020 on current projections is of a Sunday church going public of 1% of the population. One scenario is the decline of the indigenous church and the growth of immigrant church. The other is a vision of 'fragments everywhere' with various forms at various times, and 'joined-up church' where groups interlink, exchanging skills and networking around issues and styles. Prayer will be in 'nets' both digital and personal among leaders in areas who work together for a common vision. Size and customisation come together.

This is closer to New Testament community based on households and working guilds in regions of the city, held together by occasional meetings together. 'Connected fragments were the essence of the New Testament Church'.[93]

The Church as a network of networks

The early Church was about people who shaped their

lives in different ways, with different patterns of leadership, and patterns of connection through visiting, writing, praying and giving. The unity was not in being in the one place at the one time doing the one thing.

> *Meetings of congregations together, though they occurred*[94] *seem not to have been the prime vehicle of unity: these other links were more important. Communication was central. Churches were embedded in networks that were held together by networks.*[95]

This is the 'liquid church' which takes gospel shape within a given context. In the contemporary world of the mobile phone with 11.6 billion text messages on the 02 network alone, people are not even living in given networks, but in networks that are 'built as you walk'.[96]

At a Scottish Conference on this theme, Moynagh nonetheless reaffirmed the role of the local church. Place is still important. Half of adults are within 30 minutes of their mothers and see them once a week, and 42% see their fathers. While 14% of adults moved house in 1952, only 10% moved in 2002. People stay in the same place, but commute to work because both partners are working and re-location is more difficult. However, proximity does not mean community. We have lost cohesion and need to recognise the need for diversity of approach.

In that same conference he spoke of *brand church* where people gather to a church which has a distinctive flavour of worship, music, spirituality, evangelism, youth ministry or concern for social justice. These churches offer a fresh start for the many 'de-churched' of our culture, and may be ways in for the 2 million Scots who in the 2001 Census still claim some affiliation to the Church of Scotland. The issue is breaking old perceptions of church as a poor or even damaging experience at some stage in life.

The Church with a learning leadership

Leaders will act as coaches[97] to liberate people as they learn to be disciples, through the process of blessing, belonging, believing and behaving[98] to become the inside-out church.

> *The next generation of church leaders will need to include people with the gift of working with others to plant innovative forms of church. They will need to be catalysts, collaborators and coaches – not jealous of those around them, but affirming their gifts and eager to link them with other people.*[99]

The call is urgent.

> *If we remain as we are, we face near extinction in the years ahead. It is time for a church makeover, time to become a fresh church for an it-must-fit-me world.*[100]

Mission-Shaped Church[101]

From where people live to how people live

To take us further on our journey into 'fresh expressions of church' we turn again to the recent report from the Church of England called, *Mission-Shaped Church – church planting and fresh expressions of church.* Picking up from an earlier report in 1994 called *Breaking New Ground* which encouraged church planting as a supplementary strategy alongside the inherited territorial parish models, this report declares that this is no longer adequate:

> *Communities are now multilayered, comprising neighbourhoods, usually with permeable boundaries, and a wide variety of networks, ranging from the relatively local to the global. Increased mobility and electronic communications technology have changed the nature of community.*[102]

The report argues for the churches to be related to territory, neighbourhood and networks in a layered strategy of engagement. There is a place for geography and for recognisable natural communities, within which we need to take seriously the multiple networks of people-groups. We must be with people, not only '*where* they are', but '*how* they are'.[103]

Covenanted communities

This call to customise the Church carries a health warning with it. The report recognises that the consequence of this fragmentation of society is a decline in social capital. On the one hand community is being increasingly re-formed around networks and people are less inclined to make lasting commitments, but that can become 'a corrosive force that the Church must resist'.[104] The report recalls us to the covenant keeping God of the Bible by stating clearly that new initiatives must take seriously the need to plant our feet on a part of God's earth as covenanted communities – a sign of God's covenant commitment to his world:

> *Contemporary initiatives to plant the Church, or to express it appropriately within the Western culture, will need to establish social capital: ties of loyalty and faithfulness through Christ. Both the establishing of bonds within networks and the bridging between networks will be crucial.*[105]

This call to network church is not some dilettante notion that is a sell-out to consumerism. It is an attempt to be ever more faithful to the call of the Incarnation, taking on the realities of our society, but offering:

> *forms of Christian community that are homes of generous hospitality, places of challenging reconciliation, and centres of attentiveness to God.*[106]

Double listening

The Church is never shaped just by the culture but also by the tension that arises from the discipline of double listening – listening to the world around us and to the word of God coming to us in scripture and in the Christian tradition. The conversation set up by that double listening creates communities of engagement and distinctiveness.

This missionary strategy is rooted in our understanding of the nature and mission of God in creation and redemption. God is the God who loves and gives and sends, the God who creates in extravagant generosity and diversity and 'whose missionary purposes are cosmic in scope, concerned with the restoration of all things, the establishment of shalom, the renewal of all creation and the coming of the kingdom as well as the redemption of fallen humanity and the building of the Church'.[107]

Focussing on the work of Christ, the incarnation points us to a 'world to enter', the cross challenges us that there is a 'world to counter' and the resurrection reminds us that there is a 'word to anticipate'.[108]

The Holy Spirit brings to us God's creative work as 'God's gift from the future'[109], offering us a 'baptism of imagination'[110] about future forms of church.

The Trinity of Father, Son and Holy Spirit speaks of the ultimate reality being relational. God works through relationships, calling us into new covenanted relationships of interdependence through Christ in the Body of Christ. Every network both reflects and distorts this communal image of God. Every network waits to be redeemed into the fullness of the God's community of worship and be a witness to his coming Kingdom.

Territory, neighbourhood and network

Let me return for a moment to the City Centre grouping, which has been created as the basis for mission in the centre of Edinburgh. This is an attempt to create a 'mixed economy' of church life, which will allow the gathered congregations to engage with their 'multi-layered' neighbourhood and affirm within it the networks that need to entered in the name of Christ.

Across the country, churches are being asked to group together in this way to form a *parish grouping* as a new ministry area. The mission needs are assessed. The pattern of ministry team is assessed to meet those needs – a mix of the ministries, word and sacrament, youth work, administration, pastoral care, community development, paid staff and trained volunteers. In West Fife, the Benarty Parish is working to this model of team ministry. In Aberdeen, Bute, Cowal, Glasgow and Edinburgh, the parish grouping is being explored and implemented.

This model of working is undoubtedly being forced by the economics of have too few ministers for the existing parish system. But behind the move many hear the call of the Spirit to enter into a new era of collaborative ministry. This carries with it many legal challenges about ministerial tenure and congregational right of call, all of which are being debated throughout the Church at the moment. It may lead to quotas of ministers to Presbyteries. That will, in turn, require a fresh look at the patterns of ministerial formation for more specialised roles in teams, and a greater need for equipping the whole people of God to share in the mission of God as the Church in the world.

It is here that the network church comes into its own. Within these new parish groupings, where neighbourhoods are served by multidisciplinary teams from several centres of worship and mission, there will be space to identify the networks that are not touched by any of the existing bases. These networks will be lightly linked to the wider network of churches, but have a life of their own. They may be led by local leadership or enabled and equipped by others who are theologically trained to nurture the network.

In rural areas it may be that the school for the area becomes a base for youth initiatives, or one of the churches in the grouping might be stripped of its church furnishings and recreated to offer the ambience that young people enjoy, fitted with crash cushions, a food bar and multimedia equipment.

The New Charge Development in Gilmerton, which has been assigned the task of developing a 'new generation' church on the South Side of Edinburgh, has been exploring the use of the church building they have inherited. They have not been visiting other churches to steal ideas. They have been visiting the most popular pubs, clubs and cafes in the Edinburgh and Glasgow to identify the setting that help young people feel at home.

Territory, neighbourhood and network need to find ways to live together, but the power base must shift from the assumed territorial pattern to the cultural shaper of the network. That central issue of power is addressed only by the theology and spirituality of grace which pervades this book – following the way of Christ who became poor in order that we might become rich.

The test of our theology of grace will come when we move our resources of people and money to invest in neighbourhoods and networks as much as we have invested in territory.

Fresh expressions of Church

What might all this look like? It is very untidy for Presbyterians who are brought up on the creed of everything being done 'decently and in order'.

Mission-Shaped Church describes the emerging Church as 'fresh expressions of church'. These new churches which serve the networks of society take various forms:

- alternative worship communities
- base ecclesial communities
- café church
- cell church
- churches emerging out of community initiatives
- multiple congregations
- school-based or school-linked churches
- seeker churches and
- youth congregations

They have certain features in common:

- The importance of small groups for discipleship and relational mission
- They do not meet on Sunday mornings
- They relate to networks of people in business, or around schools.
- They are post-denominational
- They are connected to a resourcing network beyond the locality

St Thomas' Crookes, Sheffield

Come now to one church which has developed a pattern of church life which is both grounded both in the theology of mission which we have outlined and the social realities of the network society in which we live. The church is an Anglican church in Sheffield, called St Thomas' Crookes, where I had the privilege of interviewing some staff and members.

The Location: Philadelphia Campus

St Thomas's is located to the north of Sheffield in a clutch of units on an old industrial estate. These units offer worship space for 1,200 people, office accommodation, an online shop, a chapel and a training centre. The central buildings are about to be demolished to create a day-care nursery, an arts centre, a chapel for 100 people and a piazza, which will form a centre to the campus – known as Philadelphia because of the promise of Christ to hold before us 'an open door'.

This thriving church is set in a city which has 2% of the population attending church and is set to be the youngest city in Britain. Its focus has been to minister among Generation X, the generation missing from most of our churches. The ministry of Mike Breen over the last 10 years has built on the 27 years of Robert Warren and previous rectors. This is the fruit of 40 years of ministry – and more.

Following the contours of life

The church takes account of the contours of everyday life for this generation. Family life has broken down for many, but people are investing in friendships as the primary basis of stable relationships. The church works through networks – called 'huddles' – for pastoral support and evangelism, relating to people where they are in work or through football teams or night-clubs. People are encouraged to discover their 'life skills' as a basis of Christian living in today's society.

The huddles offer a space for mutual accountability as in the model of Wesley's class meetings. These huddles are formed into clusters of 40/50 which recognise our need for an extended family for rounded growth. The nuclear family is seen as a Western 20th century phenomenon. The extended family is the more established social pattern of other centuries and across all cultures. With the collapse of family groupings and the increase in single-person households across the UK, the clusters are intended meet the need for a wider spread of relationships. Celebrations are formed by clusters coming together for worship around focussed missional intentions. Sunday evening gatherings are specifically for teaching for the cluster leaders – 45 minutes worship, 30 minutes tea break and 45 minutes teaching – with the option to come to any one of the segments, recognising how busy people's lives can be.

The key insight is this: the church follows the basic contours of our humanity rather than forcing our humanity into predetermined contours of church structure.

Language

Language carries culture. The old language of congregation, and inherited patterns of organisation, carries within it the assumptions and images of the old world. The new order needs new language to create a new culture. The 'life skills' course (what we might describe as discipleship or Christian education) gives the church a common language of 'up, in and out' – representing worship, community building and missional activity. They embrace and encourage the five ministries of Ephesians 4:12 – apostle, prophet, evangelist, pastor and teacher.

Workplace ministry

Ann McLaurin is team vicar with a former career as a manager in Marks and Spencer. The congregation is split into four streams of young adult ministry: Expression (for students), Connect (creative arts and community), Devoted (young adults) and Radiate (for young adults in the workplace – to radiate 'the life that works').

'Radiate' exists to express the Kingdom of God in the workplace. Ann's aim is to help people treat their workplace as a community where they expect to meet God rather than a place of proactive mission dislocated from church life. The various clusters meet in different places and indifferent ways – '925' meets in Pizza Express while another group is specifically for self-employed people. The celebration for the clusters ranges between 60 and 120 people.

Teaching on Jesus at the well in Samaria has taught people to wait and pray for God's opportunities to serve or speak. The story also suggests that the village of Sychar came to recognise Jesus over a period of time. Our workplace is where we spend time. We can be patient about the outcomes.

Already people are discovering folks coming up to them and, through Alpha courses, are coming to faith in Christ. Ann has approached Marks & Spencer about meeting staff as a chaplain and has found an open door. The next stage is to take the 'life skills' course and adapt it for the workplace and offer it through the human resources section of some of the businesses.

Night-club ministry

Dave Cates is the leader of the 'Connect' celebration. One of the clusters, called D3, aims to redeem the club culture by being part of it. The club ministry began with very successful clubs of over 300 people on a Tuesday evening, but the Christian proportion increased and the contact value reduced. His team then went on the streets at 6am with water and chocolate for the dehydrated clubbers coming out of the clubs.

The group is currently small with twelve to fifteen committed people, but a larger transient group of students and others. They have good relationships with the managers, DJs and bar staff of the clubs and D3 is now city-wide with people from five churches in the city.

Currently their vision is to establish a prayer room in one of the clubs, to develop the community life of the cluster and to build on links with the self-help groups in the city – making them known through flyers distributed to clubbers.

Their larger vision is of a national network linking into

24/7 and New Generation Mission (NGM) in Bristol who have been training dancers and DJs to be in the clubs through their £3 million facility.

They intend to develop weekend events for clubbers in Sheffield with workshops, worship and mission.

The Order of Mission (TOM)

Through consultation with the bishop and others, St Thomas's was identified as being a church which is a 'resource' church with an apostolic calling. This led to various people recognising the call to establish 'The Order of Mission' for those who were called to mission in this culture.

On 6 April 2003, 'The Order of Mission' was launched as a new missionary monastic order. This is a highly disciplined missionary community and is a profound response to the missionary challenges of the times, drawing on the long tradition of missionary movements from the Celtic monasteries to the Methodists and the Salvation Army.

> *This is the tradition in which The Order of Mission (TOM) stands: a community committed under God to each other for the purpose of mission.*[111]

The members of the order are committed to each other for life: to live for God, for each other and for the world. There are clear patterns of initiation over three years, regular clusters for support and a clear pastoral leadership with the Archbishop of York as the outside Visitor to whom they are accountable.

Members of the order continue to live their lives in their own vocations in the world. Under a vow of simplicity, some work part-time in order to finance ministry in the order in the networks of society where they find themselves.

There are echoes here of the origins of the Iona Community – and some of our Celtic origins.

Key themes for network church

Affirming the people of God

We are all called to different and distinctive ministries within the one ministry of Christ in the world. The people of God are already God's agents of mission in family and daily work. The emerging Church will respect and reaffirm that vocation to follow Jesus in the everyday. The emerging Church will enable and empower people to make a difference where they are by becoming 'dispersed church' – going out but not expecting to return to the assumed base. They will need excellent resourcing.

Recovering lost ministries

Many people 'called to ordained ministry' find their core calling to such an apostolic role being frustrated by the expectations of congregational life. There is a great need to identify gifts and callings at an early stage in order to equip and deploy people accordingly. The generic training for all-embracing parish ministry will not be adequate. The variety of challenges in the networks will call for a rediscovery and reaffirmation of the full range ministries outlined in Ephesians 4 – the apostle, the prophet, the evangelist, the pastor and teacher.

We can recruit and train to support the old structures for the sake of keeping everything suitably secure and safe. Or we can deploy people to facilitate new patterns of network church in the kaleidoscopic world of the post-modern world. We need apostolic adventurers who can offer a ground-breaking call to the settled church to recover her calling to be a movement again.

Leading in chaos

In a recent lecture on 'Leading in Chaos', Professor James McNeish, a business coach and consultant, ended with these words for those of us who have to lead in chaos in business or in church:

> *You need humility, curiosity and to welcome interruptions to your way of thinking.*

These are key qualities for any kind of ministry in the world of network church.

Evangelising Scotland

This is not about the survival of the Church as we know it and love it. This is about the re-evangelisation of Scotland, and the yet-to-be Church that God already loves, but we have not yet known.

Remember ...

> *The first language to be spoken on the moon was English, but it was not somebody from England who spoke it. It was somebody from the colonies.*

Chapter Five

Exploring Post-modern Church – learning from Celts and clubbers

Lessons from a missionary

'What kind of church will offer access to the gospel for the next generation?'

My persistent question found a hint of an answer in the words of an American missionary called Vincent Donovan. After spending years among the Masai in Kenya, he applied his missionary experience to the issue of the alienated youth culture and wrote:

> *In working with young people...do not try to call them back to where they were, and do not try to call them to where you are, beautiful as that place may seem to you. You must have the courage to go with them to a place where neither you nor they have been before.*[112]

Donovan speaks of his call as missionary in Kenya:

> *I suddenly feel the urgent need to cast aside all theories and discussions, all efforts at strategy – and simply go to these people and to do the work among them for which I came to Africa. I would propose cutting myself off from the schools and the hospital, as far as these people are concerned – as well as socializing with them – and just go and talk to them about God and the Christian message... Outside of this I have no theory, no plan, no strategy, no gimmicks – no idea of what will come. I feel rather naked. I will begin as soon as possible.*[113]

These words, written in a letter to his Bishop in May 1966, as he left the security of the Roman Catholic Mission at Loliondo, express the missionary motivation that lies at the heart of this quest for new patterns of church for a new generation. We need people willing to leave the compound 'naked'!

If Donovan felt naked before he set off, he was still to experience the steady stripping of ecclesiastical and theological clothing which came from the direct missionary encounter. Such 'kenotic ministry' will be essential for our engagement with a generation untouched by the gospel:

> *A missionary is essentially a social martyr, cut off from his roots, his stock, his blood, his land, his background, his culture. He is destined to walk forever a stranger in a strange land. He must be stripped as naked as a human being can be, down to the very texture of his being.*
>
> *St Paul said Christ did not think being God was something to be clung to, but emptied himself taking the form of a slave. He was stripped to the fibre of his being, to the innermost part of his spirit. That is the truest meaning of poverty of spirit.*
>
> *This poverty of spirit is what is called for in a missionary, demanding that he divest himself of his very culture, so that he can be a naked instrument of the gospel in the cultures of the world.*[114]

His words of wisdom on how we approach the post-modern generation should be written up for all to see in every church in the land. We repeat them:

> *In working with young people ... do not try to call them back to where they were, and do not try to call them to where you are, beautiful as that place may seem to you. You must have the courage to go with them to a place where neither you nor they have been before.*[115]

The Celtic lens

My inspiration for mission in our post-modern culture has a source nearer home. My personal perspective on God, Church and mission have been influenced by the rediscovery of the Celtic Way, patterns of faith and life that shaped the Celtic Church which first evangelised these islands.

As a form of short-hand, let me introduce you to four 'Celtic couplets' which summarise that Celtic lens as a way of seeing our place in God's mission in our community.

Journey and monastery

The Celts were marked by a wanderlust and are renowned for their willingness to be on journeys to meet people where they are. The motif of the journey is vital for today's Church – to be on a spiritual journey so that we can accompany others on their spiritual journey, and to go on a literal journey to meet people where they are.

The Celtic monasteries, unlike the mediaeval monasteries of escape from the world, were the places where people were equipped for these missionary journeys – places, according to Ian Bradley, for nurturing the heart, offering a home to the stranger and acting as a hub for mission.[116] Sanctuary and hospitality are vital ministries for our buildings. However, the key lesson for us may be that buildings are not the places to which we must bring people, but places from which we send people. On that view we need fewer and smaller buildings.

Wells and monsters

The wells were places of community and often associated with magic. The Celtic Church met the people at their wells and baptised people there – making the cultural connections where people meet and affirming their own community life rather that inviting people into the monastery. Where are the 'wells' in our communities – the networks where people gather together.

The 'monsters' reminds us of Columba's legendary encounter with the Loch Ness monster, by which he freed a community from fear and won over King Brude, head of the Picts. Here is the inspiration for winning the cultural leaders – be they DJs. or club managers, or politicians or community gatekeepers – and challenging the 'powers that be' which intimidate a community.

Caim and coracle

The 'caim' is a pattern of Celtic prayer of encircling to affirm the presence of God with us and to claim his protection. That prayer can be offered on any piece of God's earth as a way of affirming it as his world and standing against the evils that invade it. It can be prayed anywhere as a prayer of presence and protection.

The coracle reminds us of the pilgrims who set off over the oceans to let the wind blow them wherever God wanted – people who were ready to risk everything to move with the Spirit and to dare to seek their place of resurrection in impossible places. The caim and the coracle encourage us to find the 'no go' areas of our community and go there.

Horse and Rider

Here is an image of contrasts. Outside a major financial establishment in Edinburgh stands a bronze statue called simply 'Horse and Rider'. It depicts a man sitting bareback on the horse, holding it by the muzzle and bending it backwards – a cruel image of control and domination. Contrast that statue with the story of gentle Aidan, the bishop of Lindisfarne, who walked everywhere on foot to be close to the poor people. King Oswald, his patron, gave him a horse for his travels. Aidan gave it away to the first poor man he met and continued on foot.

The first image is a disconcerting reminder that much evangelism is about power and control as people are manipulated into belief or into church, into our place of power. The second image speaks of the way of humility and generosity of spirit which must characterise our sharing of the good news of Jesus Christ, who though he was rich became poor so that through his poverty we might become rich – the way of grace.[117]

If you want these images restated in formal theological categories, then we are envisaging church being shaped by the *Missio Dei* and the relational foundations of the Trinity, by the vulnerable and transformative engagement of Incarnation, enjoying the liberating expansiveness of being part of God's good creation, risking the sacrificial generosity and vulnerability of the Cross while expressing the humility and quiet authority of Christ.

Church for the new generation and any generation is called to be a corporate reflection of the nature of God revealed in Jesus Christ – the true image of God. The naked missionary Church is stripped of all secondary identities to that core identity in Christ. Only then can she be re-clothed for our culture and our times.

These Celtic connections have been spelt out in a scholarly way by Ian Bradley in his *Colonies of Heaven – Celtic Christian Communities*,[118] where he recognises his own journey from romanticism to scepticism and on to an honest appraisal of practical insights and connections for our times.

In a more popular mode, but based on profound spiritual journey of apprenticeship to Celtic spirituality, Ray Simpson of Lindisfarne has written of marks of the emerging Church in *Church of the Isles – a Prophetic Strategy for Renewal*.[119] In addition to our earlier observations, he pleads for churches that are 'people-friendly and earth-friendly', centres of artistic excellence and communities of justice. These themes resonate with the post-modern pilgrims in our culture who are spiritually alert, but institutionally allergic.

The St Cuthbert's way

And so back to St Cuthbert's whose roots are in that ancient Celtic Church of 1,300 years ago. With 20,000 people coming through our parish at weekends for entertainment, the issue was how to engage the nightlife of the city. After a false start with an attempt at a Chaplaincy to a Night-club, in 1999 we commissioned research into the club scene in Edinburgh. The recommendation was to plant a Christian community in this clubbing culture and appoint a team to explore church for club culture. The project was called 'Exploring Church for Club Culture'.

It set out to answer the persistent question: 'What kind of church will offer access to the gospel for the next generation?' It was never solely a focus on the clubbing culture. We recognised the clubbing scene as a particular expression of post-modern urban culture. If we could touch this flow culture, we would find clues to the wider issues church for tomorrow.

Spirituality in club culture

Contrary to the surface view of clubbing as the arena of alcohol, drugs and sex, this social context is for many people a place of surprising spirituality. The study by David Hay and Kate Hunt of Nottingham University on *Understanding the spirituality of people who don't go to church*[120] resonates with our experience in the club scene.

They claim that there is a new spiritual openness today. The research suggests that people are 60% more likely to speak of a spiritual experience than they were in research in 1987. Our clubbing contacts have found evidence of that openness. Part of our approach has been simply to offer a context for spiritual exploration. The awareness of the 'something more' is seen in the whole musical experience of the clubs which is like a worship experience of transcendence. Many of our Christian folk go clubbing to worship. One young woman spoke of an encounter with God in the dancing which was deeper than anything she had known before.

Hay and Hunt say that people are looking for a 'quest mode' of expressing faith. That is central to our approach – even in our title which is 'exploring church for club culture' we take our place alongside people in the exploration. People discover God among people who are discovering God. Every assumption is open to question.

At the heart of the club scene is a search for intimacy – a desire for friendship that can be trusted. The Nottingham research talks about our primal 'relational consciousness' – not surprising if we believe we are made in the image of a God who is a Trinity.

Hay and Hunt call for a 'church for beginners' – but tend to assume an 'access' course approach to church as we know it. We must go further and begin to shape church around the people who are the beginners – a church of the churchless.

The most striking image in the research was the image of the 'valve', where they suggest that church in a culture of the past offered a valve that opened people to spiritual awareness. Today those same elements act as a valve to close people down. By contrast, one of our club folk was asked why this venture in club culture was so important. He replied:

> *The club culture opens people up to the spiritual awareness in ways that surprises us and people are asking us to help them.*

The club scene is one of the valves of our time. In Celtic terms, it is one of the 'wells' (a modern watering hole!) where people sense the spiritual and form community, and where our Celtic forebears went to meet people and make the well the place of Christian baptism. The club culture is a major door into 21st century urban culture.

I will come back to the cultural context later, but first, let me tell more of the story. Then the cultural comments will be less abstract.

Post-modern Church

Urban Soul

Come with me to the upstairs room of a pub in central Edinburgh. It is our first night of 'Urban Soul'. Join a small queue of people outside. Enter a makeshift tent and put on your headphones. Hear the story of the High Priest entering the Holy of Holies in the Temple at Jerusalem. Take off your shoes and enter the room. The room has dimmed lighting and ambient music. Images are projected on the walls. On the floor is a taped formation which you may or may not recognise as the Celtic sign of the Trinity. You walk inside the markings as a sign of being enfolded in the love of God.

You move from one installation to another in silence. At one stands a beautiful vase of water with a coloured light behind – an invitation to reflect on our sins and the sins of the world. We write on a piece of paper and drop it in the water. The rice paper dissolves.

You move to a group of light boxes – words on acetates to cut up and make messages to each other or to God. You barely notice but the words are from creeds and scripture – words of faith for messages of faith.

You move to a wall with images from the news of the week. In front is a bowl with stones. On each stone is taped a phrase of the Lord's Prayer. Touch the image with a stone and pray.

There are other places to visit. And then we turn to the centre. We sit on the floor around a low table with candles, bread and wine. For the first time we speak as each person says his or her name. We are a community of named people. Bread and wine are shared as a man and woman – one lay and one ordained – lead in an act of communion.

You discover people in the group of twenty people who have never been to church – or not for many years. They are asking to meet again. You reflect on the elements of the evening: individuality as each had space; mobility as people walked, sat, knelt, squatted or stood; creativity for each installation had been devised by different people; mystery as we sensed the 'something more', community as we met in the pub downstairs first, sat round the table and then lingered to chat, and continuity as the bread and wine of 2000 years was passed into the hands of people who had never handled it before, offering rootless people new connections.

Come with me again to the same place on another night. Music hits your ears long before you reach the door. 60 people are dancing to music led by a DJ and three singers. White words appear on a black sheet on the ceiling. They are strangely familiar as we find ourselves being led through a liturgy of adoration, confession and word – all involved in the dance. We pause for breaking bread and sharing wine.

The dance resumes with video-loop images on the wall of last week's news – train crashes, international conflict, funeral pyres for farm animals. A rapper calls out for justice in the world and for God to act. The body language of the people changes to anger and passion. You sense intercession as you have never sensed it before.

'Urban Soul' is our attempt to express worship in the culture of the club world. Individuality, creativity, community, connections with deep roots, mystery, body-language, image … all are present. Leonard Sweet's *Post-modern Pilgrims*[121] would find the marks of the EPIC Church – experiential, participatory, image based and connected.

Soulspace

Now come to 'Soulspace'. Here we are out of the range of the Christian people who might inhabit 'Urban Soul'. Here is an attempt to do three things: connect with the rages and dreams of urban young people, work alongside them to create music which is the life blood of the club scene, and to offer a safe space to explore pain – our own or the pain of the world. Here is the edge where we sit close to people far beyond the radar of church.

A local club gives us the space for the evening. Our musicians have met up with DJs and promoters and have devised an evening of music and dance. Our people are part of the evening. They talk around tables and at the bar. Young people ask who the band is. Connections are made. A couple of French lads ask what I do and launch into questions about Church, faith and God. I become an almost reluctant evangelist.

The safe place is no more than evenings in flats and pubs – the Church on the move meeting people where they are; offering friendship. The club scene is the culture of the bubble – the now moment. Connections that offer roots are a gift of stability. Connections that offer a space for protest at injustice offer the gift of a new future.

EH1

Now come to EH1. It is Sunday afternoon on the High Street on Edinburgh. EH1 is a cafe where clubbers meet when they wake up from Saturday evening. EH1 is where it all began and where it all connects. Over two years the team met there, meeting people and building friendships. This is the junction box as 'Urban Soul' and 'Soulspace' relate to widely different groups of people. EH1 provides the relational bridge.

The only strategy is authentic relationships. The project has had to go at the pace that relationships will bear. The team have not found it easy to work together, but there has been a commitment to truthful relationships. Truth is an expression of covenant. Only where there is truth can there be trust. Only where there is deep trust can there be a capacity for risk. Team meetings have been the best of times and the worst of times – hard things said, but deep relationships formed.

The post-modern quest is for 'the self', but the search is vain. Individualism is ultimately self-destructive and unsustainable. People made in the image of God-in-relationship must find ways to become people-in-relationship. At the simplest level this 'club church' offers people a place of an authentic friendship of truth and grace, and, in the deepest sense, 'lost souls' are found.

Rowan Williams, in *Lost Icons,* speaks of the soul in ways that are neither metaphysical nor evangelistic. He speaks of the need to use soul to describe the 'self' which comes alive only when 'it exists in the expectation of grace',[122] ultimately under the gaze of the grace of God:

> *Souls occur when trust of a certain kind occurs, the trust implied in such an invitation of the perpetually absent other ... In the background ... is the question of how much our contemporary culture nurtures or fails to nurture trust.*[123]

Whatever this journey into the club culture has been about, it has been about people discovering their souls in the gaze of grace and truth. It has been a journey of broken trust renewed. That has been the core gift of this expression of post-modern Church to post-modern people.

Reflections on club culture

Back then to the club culture. What are the cultural signals and theological connections?

1. *Club culture is a search for transcendence and intimacy.* Perhaps the club scene is more church than the Church in offering an answer to that, but we know that it is in Christ that we are led to put a face to the transcendent God who comes as Friend to lay down his life for us.

2. *Club culture is an electric and sonic culture.* 'I vibrate therefore I am' (Tex Sample)[124]. 'If I cannot dance it, can't be true' (unknown South African theologian). People pick up their messages through sound – music and the 'vibe'. It challenges us as Christ's people to embody the 'vibe' of grace and truth if we are to communicate with this culture.

Marshall McLuhan[125] claims that we have moved from left brain to right brain dominance – from sequential analysis to 'holistic pattern recognition'. This accounts for the instinctual reaction to inherited church where the 'valve' turns people off before they have analysed why. The Church is still based in the cerebral and the analytical. This culture deals in a collage of fragments. This culture is allergic to any whiff of power or control. One of our team describes normal church as 'a solo performer who dominates the community space'. Agree or disagree – that is the vibe.[126] They are hungry for that self-emptying ministry of God who, in grace, 'comes down to where we sit and listens to us there'.

3. *Club culture is a body culture.* It moves and dances. It stimulates the body with drugs and alcohol. It seeks bodily contact. The Christian gospel is 'body affirming', but inherited Christianity filtered through our Platonic classical philosophy is 'body denying'. Part of the plea of the club culture is to be free to worship and pray with our bodies. The passivity of much of our worship fails to engage them.

The story goes on

Fragile but indestructible

There is more to tell of the ups and downs of this little community which is so transient, so fragile, and yet seemingly indestructible, undergirded by the resurrection resilience of the Spirit. Four years on, the group has shrunk to about a dozen, as people have moved on to serve God in other places. But each person can speak of God moving among us in transforming grace.

Relationships of truthfulness and integrity are paramount. The emphasis lies in nurturing each other's dreams rather than canvassing support for joint projects. Communication is not by sermons or talks but by conversation round a table or through e-mail. There is a quest for godly wisdom for life on the streets. Mutual mentoring holds us to account and stimulates growth. People ask us where our teaching takes place. Everyone looks puzzled. There is not formal teaching, but we have learned a lot!

Post-modern pastoring is on the hoof. Post-modern teaching is in dialogue. Decisions are shared. Every voice is listened to. There is a cultivation of a spirituality of robust gentleness that soothes and strengthens. Whispers of tomorrow breathe into today.

Community of communities

The links with the mother church and the wider church are sustained through newsletters, cheese and wine evenings and a couple of club-team events in St Cuthbert's – one in Holy Week which was widely acclaimed and one in Advent which had a very mixed reaction. One of the issues is to move the mentality from thinking of a 'congregation plus a project', to looking at two different Christian communities who relate through meals and times of mutual reflection on the gospels – a 'community of communities'. Witness again the network church.

The Call of the Raven

This little community is now called Raven. There is a story in the name. The ravens fed Elijah when he was exhausted in his prophetic work. Jesus pointed to the ravens as signs of God's provision when we are anxious. In the mediaeval Church the raven was a symbol of the voice of the culture to the Church. In North American Indian mythology, the raven was the trickster who did unpredictable things. All these stories reflect something of the identity and nature of this little band of explorers. And to keep us from romanticising about Christian community, the collective noun for a flock of ravens is 'an unkindness of ravens' – a reminder that there is always a dark side to community life.

The Raven Trust

The whole enterprise is supported by a Trust committed to the task of fostering Christian community in the clubbing cultures of Edinburgh and encouraging people to be translators of the gospel in that culture.

The Community Flat

For almost two years the community was based in a flat in Lothian Road in Edinburgh. The place has been manned by two Guest-masters (named after Cuthbert at Ripon!) whose role has been to keep the flat open. Musicians have rehearsed. Hundreds of people have passed through for prayer weeks. Worship evenings have been hosted for a period. It has been the base for many meals and table-talk conversations. People from across the world have found a place to stay or sleep for days or months. It became a magnet for transient people looking for a Christian community that was open and welcoming.

This was no holy huddle of escapees from the urban world. This was a sanctuary where people could find their feet washed for the next stage of the journey of service in the bruising world of our city. The weekly gathering for an hour of prayer in the 'pausing place' overflowed most evenings into meals together when we shared the journeys of the week. One would be involved with asylum seekers. Another was involved with health education. Another was engaged with disadvantaged young people. Another was supported through a family suicide. Yet another sensed a call to work among the prostitutes.

Around a table the issues of life were woven together with the wisdom of God's word shared, not by any accredited teacher, but in the conversation of fellow travellers. It was a privilege to sit at that table and learn from women and men whose theological and spiritual perception always stretched me.

At this moment, after a couple of years based in a community flat, we found ourselves having to move out with no home, no money and no paid leadership. Already flats are opening up. A music and art collective is forming with around 40 people. Over the summer our weekly 'pausing place' for prayer has been on Calton Hill, and a street level church has offered a space for reflective worship. The resurrection resilience springs back with new hope. In true post-modern style we have invented more personas than Madonna!

The Monastery of Sound

At this point in time, the little community has discovered fresh energy in the dream of a project called 'The Monastery of Sound'. The dream arises from the music and art collective which has been meeting occasionally over recent months. Some of the folk are writing music that will be worship music for people in this part of our culture. Studio space has been found and funded. We expect to host regular public events for worship and reflection. A new life is emerging.

The Celtic Way

The Celtic way offered the door into this transforming encounter with the post-modern world: a creation spirituality that affirms the culture, an incarnational theology that challenges us to be in, of and for the culture, the cross and resurrection that faces any evil in the culture with courage and hope, the Holy Spirit who constantly calls us over the boundaries and, above all, the Trinity inviting us to place hospitality and relationships of integrity at the heart of all things.

A Post-modern journey

How is the gospel message communicated in this context? Let me tell you about one young man's journey to faith in Christ through this fragile little community of faith. Let me call him Gavin. Gavin is an artist. He teaches youngsters from a deprived area how to be graffiti artists. He lives a fairly basic existence.

When I first met him he was afraid to come inside our church building. He was an anarchist and churches are about power, control, patriarchy and hierarchy. He had met some other people who could not stand church as we know it, but who were struggling to be Christian in this strange world we call post-modern. (One symbol of post-modernity is a rear-view mirror. We seem to be 'post-everything'. It just means we know where we have come from, but don't know where we are going!) They spent long hours listening to his rather strange but passionate views of life and his rage at the destructive power of globalisation. They were a little community of friends committed to seeking and living the truth as they found it in Jesus.

He started to read the Bible. The creation story was his starting point. As an artist, he was fascinated by the God who creates, and who gives us the gift of creativity. He connected with a God who made things with limitless imagination. The Creation story told him he was made in the image of God. His angry search for a more just world had its roots in the passionate God of righteousness.

Next port of call was the Book of Job. For a young man who sensed the gross injustices of the world and all its pain, Job was his anti-hero. He wrote poems about Job. He wants to write a play and put it on in the Festival Fringe. God who opened Job to the mystery of life, opened Gavin to the mystery of God. If God could touch Job, then this God was worth a hearing.

Only then did Jesus come into the picture. The story of Jesus in the gospels fascinated him. Here was a role model of life lived for others – and a trouble-maker when it came to the establishment of his day. 'That's the man for me!' Gavin was ready to sign up as a follower.

But his route to a living faith is unique. How many people do you know who came to faith in Jesus Christ through reading one of the genealogies? Living in a rootless culture with a relational deficit at its heart, the genealogy of Jesus in the gospel of Luke grabbed him. Gavin traced the family tree back and back till, according to Luke, we was back with Adam, son of God. In that little phrase, Gavin recognised that Jesus had come so that he too could be a son of God. Since that time he has learned that genealogy off by heart!

Gavin became an established and valued member of our little community. He has discovered a gift for enacting poetry at the open mike sessions in pubs. Apart from his own rap poems, he has memorised sections of the book of Ecclesiastes which he performs with great passion and humour. He has found a way of relating the ancient wisdom of scripture to the issues of today.

A Personal Postscript

Personal discovery

From the outset, I have said that the persistent question has led me on a personal quest. The result may have the weakness of being subjective and unique, but the journey has led me to places of recognising the ministry of Father, Son and Spirit in ways previously unseen.

What have I learned about church for a post-modern world?

1. God is already meeting people wherever they are. Our calling is to join him.
2. The spiritual search in our culture is real, but needs new nurturing places.
3. Pain is not far from the surface – poverty, despair, loneliness, insecurity are universal.
4. People are looking for a community of relationships marked with honesty and reality.
5. Communication is by conversation that is open to question not proclamation at a distance.
6. Story is important – our story and God's story in Jesus intertwined and interacting.
7. Music, imagination, creativity, energy, mystery and history are valued.
8. When freed from church clutter to follow Jesus, we meet people who are looking for a simpler church.
9. A transformative Christian community is called to live in the tension between the poles of engagement and distinctiveness.
10. There is much to be unlearned and much more to be learned.

These few years have led me from my world of ordered

church life with its Presbyterian predictability to following Jesus among people who have taught me much about grace and honesty. They have made me ill at ease with the formalism of much church life. There have been times of deep frustration.

There were times when it seemed people would not take responsibility and 'make it happen'. I have had to learn patience and the spirituality of waiting. I have been tutored in the ministry of creating space for others. I have learned to have faith that the Church of Jesus Christ is always fragile, but indestructible. Our need for stability and security gets in the way of thriving on a spirituality of insecurity that depends only on the grace of God.

What did we get wrong that would serve as lessons for others who travel this road?

First of all our timescales were wrong. I thought that this could be set up and secured in three years. My wider experience and further reading in church planting tells me that it takes seven to ten years for a new church to reach any place of stable identity and maybe as long as fifteen years to be able to fly on its own. We need to live within the 'long rhythms of God' and avoid the seduction of instant solutions.

Our expectations for financing were wrong. The people of St Cuthbert's were hugely generous in their support of the venture, but our perspective was too short-term. We should either have secured the commitment of mother church for ten years – five years full support and five years tapered support, or else we should have taken the option of 'portfolio ministry' where there is shared responsibility within the group for financial support of the various ministries that are needed to be authentic.

Our communications were weak. The contact with the other churches has been marked by lots of good will, but there has not been the consistency that would have encouraged continuing support and mutual learning. There was some nervousness which led to a too early separation into the Raven Trust. This should have been faced and worked through more thoroughly.

We held on too long. It is almost the obverse of the earlier point, but we need to find ways of supporting the indigenous leadership to take full responsibility for the future of this little missional church. That is happening in this next phase when my role is significantly reduced from the earlier stages.

Personal role

What about my role as a minister in his fifties who is obviously no clubber!? I sum that up in two images: horse whisperer and doorkeeper. *The Horse Whisperer*[127] is a film and a novel about a horse damaged in a road accident. The normal veterinarian medicine can do so much, but not enough. The 'horse whisperer' is called in, a man who has been trained in the ways of the native American Indians to understand the language equus, who wins the horse's trust and then helps it through its fears. We need 'horse whisperer' evangelists in our time.

This is the approach of Jesus on the road to Emmaus: the stranger on the road who listened and asked the questions, who set a weekend of tragedy within the salvation history of the suffering Messiah and then disclosed himself in the hospitality of a supper table. That is the role model for evangelism today.

The doorkeeper imagery comes from Psalm 84 about being a 'doorkeeper in the house of the Lord'.[128] Those of us who are power-holders in the Church need to become permission-givers and doorkeepers who hold the doors open for a new generation to create church for a new generation – no more and no less. The new needs the old and the old needs the new in a spirit of mutual interdependence. In this time of cultural transition, the call is out for doorkeepers in a church without walls!

Covenant with the missing generation

I finish with a very personal statement which I call my 'covenant with the missing generation'. This is the final statement of my MTh Dissertation which was written in 1998, a year before this adventure began. As I read these words again, I realise how much of this covenant has come to be expressed in exploring church for club culture. For that I am grateful to God.

We promise and covenant....

It is the custom of the Church to expect people to make commitments and promises as they come to be part of the Church. This is a half truth. In keeping with the God of grace who 'first loved us', we must be the first to make promises to the missing generation as an act of grace that makes the first move in the name of Christ.

1. *We promise to meet you where you are,* literally and spiritually, and share the journey of mutual discovery to grow your own church for your generation in whatever place you feel at home. We repent of the arrogance that has imposed a uniformity that excluded you, and we renounce the arrogance that would exclude the catholicity of the wisdom of the ages for our journey together.

2. *We promise to listen and to keep on listening* beyond our settled frameworks of listening. We will listen to the rhythms of your life patterns and for your spirituality – explicit and implicit. We commit ourselves to respect the vulnerability of your unspoken pain and to offer opportunity for your unrealised potential.

3. *We promise to keep Jesus central* to all our explorations, for without him we have no identity. We repent of the secondary

issues that have made it hard for you to meet him. We have much to learn of the meaning of grace, and living the lifestyle of the Sermon on the Mount. We will travel together in small groups with Jesus at the centre, mentoring each other on the way. We will discover ways of worshipping Father, Son and Spirit that you and your children will want to share.

4. *We promise you a community where you can belong and become.* We will remember the fun factor and make festival. We will celebrate and respect the variety of temperaments and gifts you bring to worship and service. Structures will be simple, flexible and functional, consistent with the life of Christ. There will be rhythms of stillness and activity. May boredom never be your word to describe our life together. (We cannot promise you that you will never ever be bored. That would be inhuman!)

5. *We promise the challenge of living life passionately for others* and the support of others as you work out the connections of living for God wherever you are. Bring your imagination, your creativity and your passion and let's see what God can create that is beyond our asking or imagining.

6. *We promise that we will recognise Jesus Christ as the only Leader of his Church,* and we will explore together how we help each other to follow his lead. We renounce the misuse of any power and commit ourselves to the discipline of mutual listening and mutual service. Leadership gifts will be recognised from within, not imposed from outside, but we will always be accountable to the wider Church in a spirit of humility and unity.

7. *We promise to live in the grace our Lord Jesus Christ,* for we are all sinners and are bound to fail. We will live by the spirit of mutual forgiveness and refuse to hold one another bondage to the dream of an ideal. We promise to love you as you are, as far as we are able, by the grace of God.

8. *We promise to keep asking the next question ...*

Chapter Six

Ministering in the Emerging Church – the journey in, with and out

The Ministry of Grace

She sat at the piano – a little lady barely visible behind the grand piano in her cluttered front room. She taught her students to breathe. She made them warm the voice with exercises. She taught them how to place the voice for clear projection.

All around the room were photographs and press cuttings, and programmes from Covent Garden, Moscow, Rome, Tokyo, New York, Sidney Opera House – places where her students were on stage mesmerising audiences with their talent. She was not on the stage. She was at the piano in her cluttered front room.

As one who was privileged to have her tutor me for a few months for a singing project, she impressed me as the model of Christian ministry. She equipped people to express their gifts in places she would never go.

As a minister of word and sacrament, called by God to the service of the gospel, that became my dream. To gather people round the timeless story of Jesus Christ, crucified and risen, by word and sign, so that they might go and live the story, do the story and tell the story in places I would never go, as living sacraments of the love of God in the world.

That is the ministry of grace which has been our reference point throughout these chapters:

> *You know the grace of our Lord Jesus Christ, that, though he was rich, yet for your sakes he became poor, that you, through his poverty, might become rich.*[129]

Jesus Christ lived through this parabola of grace, taking that downward journey of service and obedience to death on a Cross, so that he might come alongside us, and create unique space for us to encounter God in the level plains of ordinary life and even in the dark abyss of God-forsakenness. From that place of meeting, he lifts us with him on an upward journey in a resurrection life of discovery, confidence and God-given authority. In the affirmation of that grace, we are called to share in the loving purposes of God as co-workers with God, each one gifted and called to be God's servants, God's friends, God's children.

In every age and every culture, this is the ministry of Jesus Christ in which we are called to share – called to the downward journey and to the upward journey. That downward call cuts across the grain of a culture of individualism and arrogance that believes it can construct its own reality. The upward call lifts up those who have been broken and who have been put down by the social constructs of our time.

Affirmations of ministry

As we approach our theme of 'ministering in the emerging church', let me make some affirmations about ministry:

1. Ministry in this emerging Church, as in the whole Church of all times and places, is the ministry of Christ crucified and risen.

In the words of Hebrews, we 'who share this heavenly calling' are to fix our thoughts on Jesus 'the apostle and high priest'.[130] Jesus is the one who was sent by God to be with us and who returns to God so that we may be with God. Christ leads us out to the world in apostolic mission and into the heart of God in priestly worship. Christ is the only leader. We are all followers. 'Follow me.'

2. Ministry in this emerging Church, as in the whole Church of all times and places, is the ministry of all Christ's people in the world.

Ministry is a universal calling to all Christian people to reflect the image of God in the midst of life – the image of God as seen in Christ coming not to be served but to serve and to give his life on the Cross for the salvation of the world. To minister is to serve. To serve is to be human in the image of God.

Ministry is our proper response to the God and Father of our Lord Jesus Christ as we present our bodies as a living sacrifice, and find our place and identity by his grace in the Body of Christ where we serve according to the gift of grace we have received.[131]

According to Hans Kung, 'laikos (layman) simply does not occur in the New Testament'. He maintains that there was no clergy-lay distinction until the 3rd century. Until then there was equality of status and variety of function, while the only criterion of ministry was obedience.[132]

The arena of this obedience is everyday life. The early Church was not the cluttered organisation of our day, which consumes time and energy to sustain its own life. We need to recover the dynamic flexibility of the early Church as attested by Leon Morris:

> *There was at this time a tremendous variety of ministries in the Christian Church. We cannot reduce it to any system, ancient or modern. The Holy Spirit directed the Church as he willed, with no respect for tidy human patterns, or man's demands that rules be kept.*[133]
>
> *'Flexibility is the characteristic of the early Church, a characteristic which has not always remained in later generations.*[134]

3. Ministry in the emerging Church, as in the whole Church of all times and places, includes the ministry of some whose calling is to equip all for the ministry of Christ.

In the letter to the Ephesians we are told that 'to *each* one of us grace is given … *some* are apostles, prophets, evangelists, pastors and teachers … to prepare God's people for works of service ... until we *all* reach unity in the faith ...'[135]

In the words of C K Barrett:

> *The whole Church is ministry ... all Christians are ministers ... Where they functioned properly, the churches were full of ministry; and some members were better at it, had greater natural gifts of leadership than others.*[136]

Notice how the leadership emerged from within by mutual respect and recognition. Leadership was organic and relational. The 'some' are at the service of 'all' to respect, release and empower the gift of grace in 'each'. The motivation of ministry is one of generosity – grace received and grace given.

This rescues us from the popular restricted usage of the word 'ministry'. Without grace, ministry becomes a greedy word that subtly steals the God-given role of every human being and hoards it as a special designation for a few religious professionals.

The salvation of ministry is when, like Zacchaeus, the neurotic hoarder, we are redeemed from our false securities and hand back the ministry of God to the people of God. Perhaps by the year AD 5,000, Christians will look back on a 1,700 year blip in our understanding of the Church, and indeed of our createdness! We are made in the image of God to serve God and each other as modelled for us in the example of Christ.

Having affirmed and clarified who we mean when we speak of 'ministering in the emerging Church', we turn to consider the tasks and the tone of this ministry – in both sense of living out the total ministry of Christ's people and in terms of specific roles of leadership in equipping the Church.

Our persistent question has been: 'What kind of church will offer access to the gospel for the next generation?' Our focus now is, 'What kind of ministry will equip such a church?' To answer this question, we first retrace our steps over the earlier part of the book where we have spoken of a 'church on the move', a 'post-modern parish' and 'moving towards the open ground' and we will ask: 'If this is so, then what does 'ministry' mean here?'

1. In a church on the move, ministry involves living with change and leading through transition.

Change is often experienced as loss before it is perceived as gain. People – whether young people, members or ministers – experience change in the Church as loss of the familiar landmarks of worship patterns. It has been said that the seven last words of the Church will be: 'We never did it this way before!' Many members and ministers are experiencing acute anxiety as we move into new models of being church. Solo ministry is giving way to team ministry and some feel insecure. Many feel disempowered by new expectations of communication and organisation. We know how to run congregations according to model A. We are afraid failing if we move into model B – whatever that model may be.

The irony is that, as people who believe in resurrection, we actually need not fear change. Our call is to follow Christ through death into resurrection. It is the irony of the road to Emmaus that, while the couple were blinded by their grief, the One they mourned was at their elbow. Ministering in the emerging Church will mean having the courageous hope not to lose our nerve. We cannot sail the ocean without losing sight of the shore for a long time.

Those in leadership will have to help others navigate the transition, as we would any other bereavement with its denial, anxiety, anger, yearning for the past and slow movement towards acceptance. William Bridges in his book on *Managing Transitions* speaks of three stages in transition: managing the ending well, guiding through the 'neutral zone' and making the new beginning. Using the imagery of the Exodus, he comments that, it is one step to get the people out of Egypt, but it takes longer to get Egypt out of the people.[137]

As a practical response to the shortfall in ordained ministers of word and sacrament, congregations should, as a matter of urgency encourage a policy of equipping congregational teams for worship, pastoral care and mission. Congregations can then take responsibility for being a Christian community with the support of whatever professionally trained ministers may be available.

That policy should be a regional policy of presbytery or diocese to encourage 'local collaborative ministry' within and among congregations. The gifts of each must be discerned and developed by the few for the sake of the many. If area team ministry simply results in staff teams who minister 'to and for' the people, they will fail. If they minister 'with and alongside', then the grace of God will flow to more and more people through more and more people.

2. In a post-modern parish, ministry involves telling stories and building a team.

In the post-modern parish of St Cuthbert, ministry involved three stages:

a. Pathfinder and Storyteller – walking the community and meeting the people in the area, then sharing the story of the community with the congregation through monthly sermons on the gospel of Luke. The aim was to link the missionary journey in the community with the missionary travels of Jesus, and weave these stories into the life of the congregation. If mission was to be sustainable, then 'my story' must become 'their story' embedded in 'God's story'.

b. Team-builder and Disciple-maker – building teams around key areas of activity. Work among residents and the homeless was staffed by volunteers, while the work among businesses and the night-clubs required specialist part-time staff. Team ministry is essential if we are to be the pluriform Church to touch a pluralist society. We need a matrix ministry of various skills and styles. Leadership grows out of discipleship. Future leadership was nurtured in regular courses on discipleship called 'The Journey' – and latterly a developed leadership course called 'Threshold of the Future'. Shared with my wife, this was based on the dynamic of the outward journey of strategic thinking and the inward journey of spiritual formation.

c. Community Builder and Mentor – intentional community building works through hospitality, meals and affirming people's gifts in order to create a 'community texture' of belonging. Mentoring involved a regular commitment to a fortnightly sandwich lunch with two businessmen, and a weekly Wednesday slot with two twenty-somethings. This is ministry that invests in the few. In the words of Eugene Peterson, Jesus gave himself for three years to twelve Jews in order to win all Americans!

This was only possible because we were in a team ministry. My colleague had responsibility for worship and pastoral care of the congregation. My responsibility was to develop mission strategy and build the leadership support. One shepherded within the fold. One sought the sheep not yet in the fold. Both were serving under the one Good Shepherd who in the parable leads those who are in the fold out to the open ground, and those who are out in the open ground into the folds for safety.

3. As we move towards the open ground, ministry involves increased vulnerability and leading by recognised gifting.

The Way of Cross and Resurrection

As more and more areas of the Church face the challenges of change, vulnerability will become a defining feature of the emerging Church and all who minister within it.

Once again, that is a feature of ministry which cannot be avoided, but is to be embraced as the way of grace, the way of the Cross. In Paul's remarkable manifesto on ministry in 2 Corinthians 4, we are introduced to the apostle who is very aware of his vulnerability, holding the treasure of the gospel of Jesus Christ in a 'common clay pot'.[138] He describes his experiences of being puzzled, in doubt, knocked down, and yet every time he is not destroyed. Later in the letter he describes what apostolic ministry means in terms of hardship, sleepless nights, insults, poverty, imprisonment and much more. These are not stresses of ministry from which we are to be protected. These are the stresses of missionary ministry that are to be expected.

But he sees them through the lens of the cross and resurrection of Jesus Christ. Whatever the stress factor, the resurrection resilience of the Spirit is greater. He bears the death of Jesus in himself, but the life of Christ is also being formed in him. Even more mysteriously, he writes that 'death is at work in us, but life in you'.[139] There is no other way for the grace of Christ's resurrection life to touch our nation than through the grace of Christ leading us as the Church to a place of crucifixion.

The Church in Scotland has the choice between death or death – the slow death of old age, or the decisive death of laying down our life for the next generation and for those beyond the reach of church as we know it. This crucifixion is, in the deepest sense of God's grace, necessary. This crucifixion is, in some senses, voluntary. But ultimately, the process of crucifixion is written into our history as an act done to us. None of us can crucify ourselves. Crucifixion is always at the hands of others. The grace is in the way we bear the cross and even learn to be like Christ, who 'for the joy that was set before him, endured the cross'.

In the midst of our vulnerability, the cross cannot be lifted from our backs, but we can look to the day of resurrection!

The Place of Liminality

The sharpness of that vulnerability may be seen in the experience of new charge ministry which has been described as 'trench warfare'. It involves entering new territory to live in the borderlands of the Church which others find difficult to understand. The term used is living in 'liminality' – the threshold of a culture and a church in transition. This raises massive implications for the nature of the ministry, the pressures experienced and the support systems required. This warfare has had its casualties already and the human cost can be high.

Conversations with NCD ministers are reminiscent of the concerns of UPA congregations – staffed by young, enthusiastic but relatively inexperienced ministers, operating alone in the face of immense demands and finding that the structural support systems lack the sensitivity, flexibility and generosity of resources to make life and ministry workable.

Ministry in this area of the emerging Church requires us to be able to:

1. Recruit people gifted for 'apostolic ministry' – capable of cross-cultural mission, or better still already living the gospel as a Generation Xer or Millennial in the post-modern culture.

2. Ensure that leadership is always a team of at least two or three people.

3. Identify and train (pre-and post-ordination) those who form the ministry teams.

4. Take a long view of at least ten years to relieve the anxiety of short-term expectations.

5. Cultivate a spirituality that will be sustaining and sustainable.

6. Develop a 'knack for here' through analysis, networking and spiritual discernment.

7. Recognise and negotiate the different stages of a congregation's life cycle.

8. Know that the last gift of the missionary is to leave, thus avoiding a culture of dependency.

Roles and gifts

Our inherited understanding of the ordained ministry is defined in the time-honoured phrase, ministers of word and sacrament. This description of the role of the ordained minister comes from Calvin, who with great precision wanted to address the medieval failings of ignorance and superstition. At its richest and best it describes a calling to keep Jesus Christ central to the life of the Christian community through teaching the Scriptures and celebrating the sacraments of Baptism and the Lord's Supper. We live by the story of the life, death and resurrection of Jesus. This is our core identity.

However, this definition of role is a reductionist understanding of New Testament ministry. The key that unlocked the door to 16th century reformation, may be the very key that locks the door against 21st century reformation.

In a Christendom context, the ministry of word and sacrament has come to be equated with the pastor-teacher of Ephesians 4:12. In the Christendom model, where the settled community gathers into the settled church, the settled ministry of word and sacrament as a pastor-teacher can nurture people to faith in Christ and into Christian maturity.

The challenge of our more fluid culture invites us to revisit Ephesians 4:12 and reinstate the lost callings of the evangelist, the prophet and the apostle. The evangelist shares the good news on the frontiers rather than live at the centre of the Church. The prophet listens for the word of God and discerns God's purposes in the Church and the world. The apostle is the one who is sent to pioneer and break the new ground. Of the five leadership roles, three are pointing outwards, and two pointing inwards.

In line with our earlier observation about 'each ... some ... and all', it is the role of these leaders to equip and empower others in sharing the gospel, listening and discerning God's will or being part of a church-planting team into a new neighbourhood or network. If we reinstated these outward looking leadership roles, then 60% our church life would be geared to looking outwards and only 40% inwards. Compare that with a time budget on most church programmes!

In our mission field of Scotland we need all the gifts to present the fullness of Christ who was the apostle, prophet, evangelist, pastor and teacher. To be the body of Christ we need to discover God's call: Let my people grow![140] Let my people go – in apostolic mission. Let my people hear – in prophetic discernment. Let my people share – in evangelistic conversation. Let my people care – through pastoral community. Let my people learn – through being apprenticed to the story of Jesus Christ.

The Journey in, with and out

Ministers the Church wants ...?

Up to this point, we have been addressing the emerging Church as an evolution within our congregational understanding and experience of church. In pursuing our persistent question about church for the next generation, chapters four and five explored network church and the post-modern church as more radical examples of the emerging Church for an emerging culture.

In our reflections on ministry, up to this point we have been talking in recognisable terms about incremental changes involved in ministering in the emerging Church. At this stage we need to change gear!

'The ministers the Church wants are ...'

When a friend used these words in a conversation, it became clear to me that we may be facing a watershed. If we select ministers that the Church wants, we may end up with the Church we have always had – the one that most other people do not seem to want! Instead of asking what ministers does the Church want, it may be that we need to ask what kind of ministers of the gospel does our culture need?

New generational leaders

We use the phrase, 'thinking out of the box'. The fallacy of that description is that there is a 'box' to think out of! Those of us who have been socialized in the inherited Church have a 'default position' to which we return. Ministry in the emerging Church will mean actively seeking and equipping people whose default position is the post-modern world, the Generation X and Mosaic generations.

The generational distance is a crucial issue for us. Our ministers are getting older. The age profile of our eldership places 10% over 75, 56% between 57-75, 30% between 35-56 and only 3% under the age of 35.[141]

To engage the rising generation we require to identify leaders under 35 (so-called Generation X) and find ways of assessing, authorising and releasing them to be leaders in their generation while they are still in touch with it. A recent New Charge Development conference for potential new charge ministers revealed students who had a passion for this kind of ministry, but who found their dreams suppressed in the process of training within the inherited modes.

We must not socialize them out of the emerging culture. The challenge for those of us who have responsibility for future ministers is to take the downward way of grace that will enable them to take the upward journey of affirmation, recognition and authorisation to minister in this culture in new ways for a new generation.

To make the point, we will leave Scotland for a moment to listen to two American voices of people who are living out patterns of ministry that relate to the contours of this emerging culture.

They will introduce us to a pattern of ministry which may be described as the journey 'in, with and out'. This is a pattern for 'all' in the body of Christ and for the 'some' who are called to roles of leadership in a range of specific ministries.

Covenant Community Church

Jud Hendrix is the pastor of Covenant Community Church, Louisville, Kentucky. For five years he and a female colleague have been co-pastoring an innovative church for post-modern people within the Presbytery of Louisville. Compared with other new church developments in the Presbyterian Church (USA), this touches a modest number of people (around 50-70 at worship), but has created an environment where every person's gift is affirmed as a gift for ministry and that gift is related to a pattern of engagement in the world – from supporting vulnerable young mothers to tackling issues of global poverty.

Their focus is to embody and envision God's shalom of justice for God's world. They hold together a theology of God's transcendence in mystery and God's immanence in the person of Jesus of Nazareth. Every one who associates with them is invited to join the 'missional dance'. They are introduced to missional groups where they are helped to find their life's calling in the world. There is a regular gathering for theological reflection which meets in a pub called 'Theology on Tap'. They work towards building 'intentional community'.

Worship connects people with God and their everyday world by involving people from the 'missional clusters' so that the stories of that group are part of the worship. Worship is a verb not a noun.

In, with and out

They gather round God's call to follow Jesus in the world and define their ministry by the three simple prepositions: in, with and out. ***'In'*** refers to the ministry of prayer, contemplative and intercessory. ***'With'*** refers to their communal life together as a shared ministry in the body of Christ. ***'Out'*** refers to their mission focus.

Each of these groups is led by pairs of people who rotate every three months. There are no solo leaders, and no fixed positions. That way the power dynamics are never allowed to solidify. Those who oversee the 'in' dimension offer support in spiritual direction and prayer accompaniment. Those who facilitate the 'with' dimension are responsible for hospitality and community-building through good communication links. Those who facilitate the 'out' dimension ensure that the groups do not lose their healthy focus on serving in God's world.

Ministry in the background

The role of the two ordained pastors is in the background. They do not lead worship or any of the groups. They offer a supporting ministry for the rotational leadership through workshops on theological and practical themes. This is upside-down church and ministry.

When I heard this story at a conference in Atlanta in October 2003, my heart leapt. Here was a clearly developed pattern of post-modern church life that our little Raven group seemed to be fumbling towards. Moreover, here was an experimental church authorised within the Presbyterian system. Here was the truly upside-down church where the mission of God is the primary focus, the people of God exercise the primary ministry and the ordained pastors are the support workers that others may flourish in Christ.

Here was the ministry for the emerging Church in three words: in, with and out. The simplicity cut through much verbiage and confusion – echoing the metaphor of the Celtic monastery nurturing the heart for God, offering a home to friend and stranger and becoming the hub that equips people for the missionary journey of life in God's world. In, with and out. Heart, home and hub. Simple!

Emerging values in the emerging culture

Brian McLaren is pastor in Cedar Ridge Community Church in Maryland and a Fellow in a movement called Emergent Village. His writings are being devoured by people who are tired of all the analyses about failing church and the culture wars, but who want the wisdom of one who is walking the talk of church for this emerging generation.

In an article in *Leadership* Magazine[142] he speaks of the 'Emerging Values' in the next generation which will shape ministry among them. He speaks of the 'spiritual formation stream', the 'river of authentic community' and the 'missional current'.

He could have used the three words 'in, with and out'! We will use his framework to unpack some of the elements of ministry in this context.

The spiritual formation stream

People are not looking for belief systems to sign up for, but looking for 'Christianity as a way of life', or 'Christianity as a path of spiritual formation'. He asks the question: 'If you were to live another thirty years, what person might you become?' That is a challenging call to long-term discipleship in a short-term culture.

For those of us who are involved in (and even love!) preaching, it means that preaching 'steps down from its pedestal to join the singing, the Lord's Supper, prayer, silence and recitation as one formative ritual among many'.[143] The new ministry is the liturgist who is an artist drawing from ancient and contemporary streams weaving a texture for group spiritual formation.

McLaren's words echo with the wisdom of Henri Nouwen in *The Wounded Healer.* Writing almost 30 years ago, Nouwen struggled to express how to minister among a 'fatherless and convulsive generation'. He saw the need for people who can be interpreters of the inner landscape of the spiritual journey:

> *The first and most basic task required of the minister of tomorrow is to clarify the immense confusion which can arise when people enter this new internal world. It is a painful fact indeed to realise how poorly prepared most Christian leaders prove to be when they are invited to be spiritual leaders in the true sense ...*
>
> *The key word here is articulation ... The Christian leader is, therefore, first of all, a person who is willing to put his own articulated faith at the disposal of those who ask for help. In this sense he is a servant of servants, because he is the first to enter* the promised but dangerous land, *the first to tell those who are afraid what he has seen, heard and touched.*[144]

I believe that those of us who are to tell the gospel story in our time must go through a double movement. First we must incarnate the word by which God is addressing us. Christian leaders will let God write on our hearts and lives the truth God wants people to know. That is the first painful journey. The second is equally tough. It articulates that truth in fresh language and imagery, minting the currency of the eternal gospel in coinage that speaks heart to heart as well as mind to mind. In that way the seed of the eternal Word is carried beyond the path, the rocks and the thorns to take root in good soil.

The River of authentic community

McLaren points out how community is broken up by our dependence on cars, our manic pace of life and our transience which means that 'right about the time we, against all the odds, get close to a circle of friends, half of them will up and move away'.

> *Throwing a small-groups programme at this hunger for community is like feeding an elephant Cheerios, one by one. What is needed is profound reorganisation of our way of life, not a squeeze-another-hour-for-community into the week.*[145]

He begins to imagine a recovery of a monastic movement of hospitality, where a few people in our churches practise radical hospitality and generous community. Homes become places of warmth and welcome for people for whom home may have become an unstable or even an abusive place.

In this context, the leader of the community is no longer the teacher, therapist, manager or hero/martyr of corporate church.

> *'Community leaders in the emerging culture will increasingly resemble the* lead seeker *in a journey, not possessing all the answers, but possessing a contagious passion to find a way home – and to bring others along*

in our common search for love, courage, wisdom and home.'[146]

Henri Nouwen anticipates this pattern of life-giving leadership when he speaks of the need to move from hostility to hospitality, from seeing strangers as enemies, to seeing them as potential friends by making the first move of grace towards them. Hospitality is an attitude that flavours life, not simply the open door of our homes.[147] In the transient world where there are no roots to the past, the gift of hospitality gives the gift of rock-like stability in an uncertain liquid world.

The Missional current

Missional is the current language for missionary engagement, blending the confrontation of mission with the alongsided-ness of relationship, integrating ecology, reconciliation, community engagement, evangelism and plain ordinary kindness in everyday living.

The old mission language defined those who were 'in' and those who were 'out', drawing firm boundaries of definition. Missional Christianity sees God expressing his love to everyone through our acts of kindness and invites others to join in the mission. On the way, as we travel shoulder to shoulder, they too may find God.

Here is the attraction of pragmatism for Generations X and Y. They want to make a better world. By acting as if we believe in a God who wants a better world, they begin to recognise this God for themselves.

Core spirituality

We have stayed with these themes of 'in, with and out', for they represent the core spirituality, not only of this culture, but of any culture. These movements are in tune with the fundamental spirituality of being human. While Christians may want to insist on the God who is 'beyond' as well as 'in', the 'in' of this triad is not about narcissism. It is about entering into the mystery of God, transcendent and immanent, through the grace of Jesus Christ by the Holy Spirit.

Donal Dorr's reflections on 'Integral Spirituality' are based on Micah's timeless description of God's requirements for being truly human: 'To do justly, to love mercy and to walk humbly with your God.'[148] Dorr sees these as overlapping responses to God: socio-political justice (do justly), interpersonal relationships (love mercy) and personal responsibility (walk humbly with God). These might be described as 'out', 'with' and 'in'.

When Jesus challenged the religious leaders of his day about their spirituality, he reminded them that the core spiritual issues were justice, mercy and faith.[149] Paul describes the dimensions of true humanity in terms of an eschatological shakedown. When all else has gone, these three remain: faith, hope and love – faith in God, love for one another and hope in God's new creation.

Ministering in the emerging Church means learning, by the grace of God, to become fully human. Any one of us may be the 'lead seeker' on the journey 'in', 'with' and 'out'. This is the ministry of God's people lived out in family, work, leisure, community and politics. This is the core spirituality to be cultivated among those who are called to offer leadership among the people of God in this generation.

Equipping leaders for the emerging Church

The question that remains is: how do we equip people to minister in this emerging Church?

Cross cultural mission

Mission-Shaped Church begins its proposals on leadership and training with this recommendation:

> *The initial training of all ministers, lay and ordained, within the Church of England should include a focus on cross cultural evangelism, church planting and fresh expressions of church. This should be a significant feature of Continuing Ministerial Education (CME) from ordination through to years 3 and 4.*[150]

The Australian writers, Frost and Hirsch, in *The Shape of Things to Come*, outline some of the skills needed for ministry in this pioneering context:

- A more actional approach that directly develops distinct entrepreneurial skills
- A sharpened ability to interpret and engage popular culture, as opposed to church culture
- Capacities to implement marketing-type strategies
- Skills in basic sociological research and in the interpretation of general social trends
- Innovative evangelistic communication skills, including 'media awareness' and leadership and team development skills[151]

These points illustrate the focus that is required to our training if we are to prepare missional leaders for the 21st century.

Pioneer training

The Church of England recognises that pioneer church planters learn by doing and by socialization rather than by formal learning. They are action-orientated and problem-solvers. Taking those with the passion and the gift for missional leadership out of the local situation into academic institution either frustrates them or, even worse, blunts their passion and gifting.

Bob and Mary Hopkins[152] of the Anglican Church Planting Initiative have proposed a parallel track for missional leadership that combines three elements:

1. the non-formal learning of tasks that include working in a community/network to plant a fresh expression of church,

2. the socialization factor of being rooted in a missional church, mentored by a missional leader, and

3. the formal teaching through distance learning and residential schools.

Learning network

Recently those who are involved in church planting in the Church of Scotland have formed a learning network to offer four times a year a 24 hour period for spiritual refreshment and formation, skills training focussed on practical issues, and conversations around wider theological and strategic themes. Two of the events are hosted in New Charges, and we reflect on the stories of these emerging churches with the help of a theological reflector. Two of the gatherings are residential and include periods of retreat, prayer and mutual support.

This is one practical response to the need to nurture a new generation of leadership for a new generation of church ministry and mission.

Portfolio ministry

However, it would be wrong to end with a focus only on those who are called to full time ordained ministry. There are many who are called to church planting who will never travel that route. We are seeing fresh patterns of missionary response today.

We live in the age of 'portfolio working' when people earn a living on two or three part time jobs. Some Christians in the Generation X category see their calling to serve Christ in the world through specific Christian ministries, but they work part-time in order to support that ministry. We might call this 'portfolio ministry'.

That assumes certain life-style choices about simplicity of living, but part of the Generation X critique of church life is that we have become too sophisticated and ministers have priced themselves out of the mission-field. We might speak of 'tent-making' or 'bi-vocational' ministry, but we must find ways of recognising those who have this calling and offering opportunities of service and appropriate training.

Urban expression

In East London, 'Urban Expression' is a small Baptist organisation committed to offering Christian witness in under-churched areas. They recruit people with a passion for living and sharing the gospel on the basis of 'no salary, no house and no deacons'. Teams of up to seven people are placed in areas and asked to find their own resources – usually through 'portfolio working' – and given mentoring support. There are discussions underway to introduce this as a possible option into Glasgow. That will be one way of exploring new models of training for the future. We need many more.

The Church for the next generation will raise up new patterns of leadership and new ways of equipping them in spiritual formation, community building and missional effectiveness.

Conclusion

In this book we have wrestled with the persistent question: What kind of church will offer access to the gospel for the next generation? The responses have undoubtedly raised even more questions. Live with the questions of the unfinished kingdom and trust the Spirit for the next step.

We end with the wise words of Archbishop Oscar Romero:

This is what we are about. We plant seeds that one day will grow. We water seeds already planted, knowing that they hold future promise.

We lay foundations that will need development. We provide yeast that produced results far beyond our capabilities.

We cannot do everything, and there is a sense of freedom in realizing that. This enables us to do something, and do it well.

It may be incomplete, but it is a beginning, a step along the way, an opportunity for the Lord's grace to enter and do the rest

We may never see the end results, but that is the difference between the master builder and the worker.

We are workers, not master builders; ministers, not messiahs.

We are prophets of a future, not our own.

A Hope Unfulfilled?

Chalmers' Legacy

At the funeral of Thomas Chalmers, Dr Lindsay Alexander spoke of the great man's ministry in the West Port among the poorest people of Edinburgh:

> *"(he) left behind him his West Port experiment as a monument of what was possible, and as an encouragement to all future generations to continue to cherish what had proved to him – a hope unfulfilled."*[153]

"A hope unfulfilled" does not mean disappointment. These words accurately describe all ministry and mission in God's Kingdom, already among us and yet still to come. The Risen Christ stands on the horizon beckoning us to follow him over the next hurdle, and daring us to anticipate the New Creation in the here and now. We are to be a sign of what God is yet to do, a bush set alight with the fire of lightning from far beyond us. As Oscar Romero said, "we are prophets of a future not our own."

The themes we have explored in this book are all to be found in the life and ministry of Thomas Chalmers. His passion was for the Christian good of Scotland and a Church committed to the spiritual welfare of the nation. He showed a genius for shaping the Church's structures to meet the missionary challenges of urbanisation and industrialisation. He was personally committed to the poorest people of Scotland right to his last breath. He would applaud today's focus on mission.

He motivated the Church of his time to open 200 new churches in four years (1834-38) at the cost of £200,000, financed by "dukes and ditchers", long before the flurry of building by the Free Church of Scotland after 1843. For him the population was shifting and the Church had to move to be where the people were. Today the population is not shifting physically, but it is shifting culturally, and the urgency to be alongside the people is just as great today as then.

Amidst the questions and anxieties facing contemporary ministry, it is worth recalling that Chalmers' perception and pattern of ministry changed dramatically during his life-time, but through it all he was sustained by the conviction that the Gospel of Jesus Christ "was the one great force through which all things might be made new."[154]

In the hands of God, hope would not remain unfulfilled.

Holding to that hope is not easy. Not only do the facts fight against our faith, but there are times when the internal landscape of faith changes so dramatically that we lose our bearings. Biblical images of wilderness, desert and exile come to mind, bringing us courage from the knowledge that the people of God have been here before. Chalmers himself used the same metaphor:

> *"I live as if in exile from God, in a dry and thirsty land where no water is."*[155]

It is with that metaphor of exile that we must learn to live today.

Living through exile

All statistical trends indicate the same conclusion: the Church of Scotland is set to become older, smaller and poorer. This is not a statement of Presbyterian predictability or some kind of theological determinism. This is a description of a transition zone for our Church and our culture.

My call to Christ and my call to ministry were both grounded in the story of the call of Jeremiah. That dramatic calling to the young prophet was in terms of destroying and uprooting and then building and planting. His prophecy was first a preparation for exile and then words of hope to endure the exile.

Looking back on 40 years as a disciple of Christ and 30 years of ministry, I recognise this paradigm at work in our time. We have been living through a time of dismantling, but I dare to believe we are entering a time of building and planting. The church is a procession of people with some still in the dismantling phase, some experiencing the disorientation of exile, while others are moving into the creative phase of new beginnings.

In terms of bereavement counselling, we are told that we move through various stages of grief over a prolonged period of time. The final stage – according to one analysis – is the moving of emotional investments from the past to the future.

As a Church, we are in mourning for a past that is behind us. Some are in denial. Some are experiencing the pain and feel the anxiety, anger and yearnings for the past, that go with that pain. Others have reached a stage of acceptance that the past is gone. An increasing number are recognising that we are moving into a new future and that it is time to "move the investments" – emotional and literal – to the future.

Like the disciples on the Emmaus Road, mourning the loss of their friend and their future, we live with the irony that the One we mourn is at our elbow. That is all we need to continue the journey.

With that perspective, we turn to face the reality of where the Church in Scotland is – but in a spirit of hope and expectation, not in a spirit of fear.

The Church of Scotland may be smaller, older and poorer. It is a distinct possibility that its capacity for national coverage to offer the grace of God to all will dry up in the next 20 years – unless we learn to work in partnership with other churches to fulfil the vision, decide to plant new generation churches alongside the old, and liberate the people of God to share in the mission of God in the nation and beyond. If we have the grace and courage to do these things we may "beat history", by creating an alternative future.

In the meantime, we could do no better than read and re-read Jeremiah's pastoral letter to the exiles in Babylon. Timid prophets claimed that the crisis would blow over and they would return quickly to the familiar world of Jerusalem. By contrast Jeremiah calls for courage, patience and hope - to settle down for the long haul of three generations, to seek the welfare of the strange city where they lived, and rediscover the deep longing for God that had been buried beneath the rubble of old religious routines.

It may take another generation or two to unlearn the Christendom models of church which are burned into our bones and our brains, but by the unfailing grace of God revealed in Jesus Christ, we will discover God in new and unexpected ways:

> *"For I know the plans that I have for you, declares the Lord, plans to prosper you and not to harm, plans to give you a hope and a future. Then you will call upon me and come and pray to me and I will listen to you. You will seek me and find me when you seek me with all your heart. I will be found by you, declares the Lord."*[156]

That hope will not go unfulfilled.

Notes and acknowledgements

Foreword

[1] 'As a national Church representative of the Christian Faith of the Scottish people it acknowledges its distinctive call and duty to bring the ordinances of religion to the people in every parish of Scotland through a territorial ministry.'

Introduction

[2] Edwards, David L, *The Futures of Christianity*, Hodder and Stoughton, 1987, p 13
[3] Blaikie, W Garden, *Thomas Chalmers*, Oliphant, Anderson and Ferrier, Edinburgh, 1896, p 142
[4] p 55 – quoting Thomas Chalmers
[5] Ibid. p 147

1. Church on the Move

[6] Brierley, Peter, *Turning the Tide – the Challenge Ahead, Report of the 2002 Scottish Church Census,* Christian Research, 2003
[7] Christian Research Association, *Quadrant Magazine*, September 2001
[8] Riddell, Mike, Pierson, Mark, Kirkpatrick, Cathy, *The Prodigal Project: Journey into the Emerging Church*, SPCK, 2000, p 1
[9] Mead, Loren, *Transforming Congregations for the Future*, Alban Institute, 1994, p ix
[10] The facts and observations in this section were collated in the research period of the Special Commission anent Review and Reform (1999-2001) which reported to the General Assembly in 2001. It is not possible to reference them more specifically.
[11] Isaiah 43:19
[12] *The Prodigal Project*
[13] Colossians 1:16

[14] A phrase used by Dr John Drane during a conference on engaging with the Bible through the creative arts.
[15] Giles, Richard, *Repitching the Tent – reordering the church building for worship and mission*, Canterbury Press, 1999
[16] Social Capital Report, Glasgow Urban Studies Unit, *Report of the Board of Social Responsibility, Reports to the General Assembly of the Church of Scotland*, 2003, pp 11, 19-21
[17] Brierley, Peter, *Future Church – a global analysis of the Church to the year 2010,* Monarch and Christian Research, 1998, p 41
[18] Unsourced quotation
[19] Taken from a seminar in The Parish Church of St Cuthbert, September 1999
[20] Bradley, Ian, *Colonies of Heaven – Celtic Christian Communities*, Northstone, 2000, pp 1-57
[21] Storrar, William, *Democracy and Mission, in God and Society*, ed. Storrar W and Donald Peter, St Andrew Press, 2003, p 11
[22] Blount, Graham, *A New Voice in a New Land?* Ibid. p 37
[23] p 19
[24] p 18
[25] Hassan, Garry, *The Anatomy of the new Scotland – power influence and change*, title essay in the book of the same name, ed Hassan, Garry and Warhurst, Chris, Mainstream Publishing (Edinburgh), 2002

2. Living with Questions

[26] In 1997 The Church of Scotland Department of National Mission presented a report to the General Assembly entitled *Beyond Barriers to Belief (1997 Reports pp 17/53-58).* This report was based on a detailed survey of 78 congregations across Scotland and highlighted key elements in the lifestyles of congregation that were growing numerically. Although the report was intended for full discussion in congregations, it did not go beyond the consideration of Presbytery committees. In terms of clues to internal renewal it offers significant starting points.
[27] Acts 18:9-10
[28] Colossians 1:27
[29] Wendell Berry, the farmer-author, quoted in Bennison, Charles E, *In Praise of Congregations,* Cowley Publications, 1999, p 214

[30] Schreiter, Robert, *Constructing Local Theologies*, London SCM Press, 1991, p 2
[31] For information on St Cuthbert's see www.st-cuthberts.net
[32] *Premium*, Scottish Provident Group, Issue No 35, Dec 1997
[33] For information on Oasis see www.oasisedinburgh.com and www.businessalphaedinburgh.com
[34] For information see www.ravenonline.net
[35] Moltmann, Jurgen *Theology and Joy*, SCM, 1973, p55
[36] Middleton J. Richard and Walsh,Brian J, *Truth is Stranger than it used to be: Biblical Faith in a Post Modern Age*, SPCK, 1997, p 61
[37] Nouwen, Henri, *Reaching Out,* Fount, 1987, pp 94-102
'Once we have given up the desire to be fulfilled, we can offer emptiness to others. Once we have become poor, we can be a good host. It is indeed the paradox of hospitality that poverty makes a good host. Poverty is the inner disposition that allows us to take away our defences and convert our enemies into friends.' p 95
[38] Ward, Pete, *Liquid Church,* Hendrickson and Paternoster, 2002, p 30
[39] Hinton, Jeanne and Price, Peter B. *Changing Communities – Church from the Grassroots*, Churches Together in Britain and Ireland, 2003, p 12
[40] Paper presented by Dr Dominic Smart, minister of Gilcomston South Church, Aberdeen, at the Annual Conference for New Charge Development in November 2002
[41] 2 Corinthians 8:9
[42] John 1:14
[43] Acts 1:8
[44] Hauervas S and Willimon WJ, *Resident Aliens*, Abingdon Press, 1989, p 59
[45] Acts 15:11
[46] Acts 15:19
[47] Kung, Hans, *The Church*, p130

[48] Brierley, Peter, *Turning the Tide – The Challenge Ahead, Report of the 2002 Scottish Church Census*, Christian Research Association, pp 106-7
[49] Ibid. p 116
[50] Hilborn, David and Bird, Matt, *God and the Generations – youth, age and the Church today*, Paternoster Press, 2002
[51] Brierley, Peter, *Turning the Tide – the challenge ahead*, Christian Research, 2003, p 58
[52] McIntosh, Gary, *Making Room for the Boom, or Bust: Six Models of Reaching Three Generations*, Fleming H Revell, 1997
[53] Adapted by Colin Sinclair for a seminar in preparation for Mission Scotland's School of Evangelism, January 2003
[54] Dougall, Neil, *Two Generations Adrift in Rutherford Journal Vol 10, No 2*, Autumn 2003, p 5
[55] McLaren, Brian D., *The Church on the Other Side*, Zondervan, 2000, p 19
[56] Sweet, Leonard, *Soul Tsunami – sink or swim in new millennium culture*, Zondervan, 1999
[57] Ibid. p 17
[58] Sweet, Leonard, *Post-modern Pilgrims – First Century Passion for 21st Century World*, Broadman and Holman Publishers, Nashville, 2000
[59] Ibid. p 2
[60] Ibid. p 47
[61] Ibid. p 46
[62] Ibid. p 56
[63] Ibid. p 92
[64] Ibid. p 109
[65] John 15:12
[66] Ibid. p 127
[67] Quoted by William Storrar in an unpublished paper to the Coordinating Forum of the Church of Scotland, March 2000
[68] Reports to the General Assembly of the Church of Scotland, Panel on Doctrine, 2002, p 13/13
[69] Ibid. p 13/14

[70] Roxburgh Alan J. *The Missionary Congregation, Leadership and Liminality*, Trinity Press International, 1997 p 23 – a term to describe living through the transitional phases of life and used to describe ministry in times of transition.

4. Network Church

[71] Sweet, Leonard, *Soul Tsunami*, Zondervan, 1999
[72] Hinton and Price p 17
[73] Jeremiah 1:10
[74] Isaiah 28:16
[75] Newbigin, Lesslie, *The Open Secret*, London, SPCK, 1978, p 1
[76] Ibid. p xi
[77] Ibid. p 29, quoting Rev Bob Hopkins of the Anglican Church Planting Initiative
[78] Ibid. p 40
[79] Ibid. p 85 quoting Tim Dearborn
[80] Ibid. p 116
[81] Thwaites, James, *Church beyond the Congregation: The strategic role of the Church in the post-modern era*, Paternoster Press, 1999
[82] p 37
[83] p 45
[84] p 45
[85] Proulx, Annie, quoted in Giles, Richard, *Re-Pitching the Tent – Re-ordering the church building for worship and mission*, Canterbury Press, 2000, p 3
[86] p 289
[87] Moynagh, Michael, *Changing World – Changing Church*, Monarch, 2001
[88] p 16 – for full details of the project and its process of consultation of interviewing 200 experts,10 two-day consultations, and distribution to 50,000 decision-makers in May 2000.
[89] p 16
[90] p 70
[91] p 86
[92] p 96
[93] p 106
[94] 1 Corinthians 14:23

[95] p 140
[96] These two paragraphs are drawn from the NCD Conference with Michael Moynagh in November 2003.
[97] p 172
[98] p 173
[99] p 188
[100] p 190
[101] *Mission-Shaped Church – church planting and fresh expressions of church in a changing context*, Church House Publishing, 2004
[102] Ibid. p xi
[103] p 12
[104] Ibid. p 7
[105] p 7
[106] p 13
[107] p 85
[108] p 87-8
[109] p 89
[110] p 90
[111] *The Order of Mission – an introductory guide*

5. Exploring Post-modern Church

[112] Donovan, Vincent J, *Christianity Rediscovered: An Epistle from the Masai,* SCM, 1982, p vii
[113] Ibid. p 15
[114] Ibid. pp 193-4
[115] Donovan, Vincent J, *Christianity Rediscovered: An Epistle from the Masai*, SCM, 1982, p vii
[116] Bradley Ian, *Colonies of Heaven: Celtic Christian Communities,* Northstone, 2000, pp 1-57
[117] 2 Corinthians 8:9. This is the only definition of grace we are given in all of Scripture.
[118] Bradley, Ian, *Colonies of Heaven – Celtic Christian Communities,* Northstone Publishing, 2000
[119] Simpson, Ray, *Church of the Isles – a prophetic strategy for renewal,* Kevin Mayhew, 2003

[120] Hay, David and Hunt, Kate, *Understanding the Spirituality of People who don't go to Church – a report on the findings of the Adults' Spirituality Project at the University of Nottingham,* August 2000
[121] Sweet, Leonard, *Post-modern Pilgrims – first century passion for the 21st century world,* Broadman and Holman Publishers, 2000
[122] Williams, Rowan, *Lost Icons – Reflections on Cultural Bereavement,* Continuum, London/New York, 2003, p 215
[123] *Op Cit* p 215
[124] Sample, Tex, *The Spectacle of Worship in a Wired World: Electronic Culture and the Gathered People of God,* Nashville: Abingdon Press, 1998, p 84
[125] McLuhan, Marshall, *The Medium and the Light: Reflections on Religion,* Toronto: Stoddart Publishing, 1999, p 53
[126] I owe the comments and references 13 and 14 in this paragraph to the work of Paul Thomson, one of the staff team, in an essay entitled, *God in 3D – Technology and Religious Imagination in Club Cultures* as part of his MTh on The Theology and Ethics of Communication. Paul is the real theologian of the team.
[127] Evans, Nicholas, *The Horse Whisperer,* Corgi Books, 1998
[128] Psalm 84:10

6. Ministering in the Emerging Church

[129] 2 Corinthians 8:9
[130] Hebrews 3:1
[131] Romans 12:1
[132] Kung, Hans, *The Church,* p 125
[133] Morris, Leon, *Ministers of God,* IVF, p 69
[134] Ibid. p 90
[135] Ephesians 4:7,11,12
[136] Barrett, CK, *Church, Ministry and Sacraments,* pp 30, 38
[137] Bridges, William, *Managing Transitions – making the most of change,* Nicholas Brealey Publishing, 2001, p 37
[138] 2 Corinthians 4:7
[139] 2 Corinthians 4:12
[140] Harper, Michael, *Let my People Grow – Ministry and Leadership in the Church,* Hodder and Stoughton, 1977

[141] Statistics obtained from research by The Rev Graham Duffin, Loanhead
[142] McLaren, Brian D *Emerging Values: The next generation is redefining spiritual formation, community and mission, in Leadership Summer 2003, Vol XXIV, Number 3*, p 34
[143] p 36
[144] Nouwen, Henri, *The Wounded Healer*, Image Books, 1979, p 37
[145] McLaren p 38
[146] Ibid. p 38
[147] Nouwen, Henri, *Reaching Out – Three Movements of the Spiritual Life*, Collins Fount, 1987, pp 94-101
[148] Micah 6:8
[149] Matthew 23:23
[150] *Mission Shaped Church*, p 147
[151] Frost, Michael and Hirsch, Alan, *The Shape of Things to Come – Innovation and Mission for the 21st Century Church*, Hendrickson Publishers, 2003, p 219
[152] Hopkins, Bob and Mary, *Towards Pioneer Missional Leadership – a pilot project for new selection, training and deployment processes*, Anglican Church Planting Initiative *www.acpi.org.uk*

A Hope Unfulfilled?

[153] Blaikie, W Garden, *Thomas Chalmers,* Oliphant, Anderson and Ferrier, Edinburgh , 1896, p 160
[154] p 104
[155] p 89
[156] Jeremiah 29:11-13

Printed in the United States
56860LVS00003BA/190-198